Time to Refine:

A STRONG Woman's Guide to Retiring on Her Own Terms

By Jessica Weaver

To Sue,
Thank you for your
trust & support! Cheers
to your next chapter.

♡ Jess

Time to Refine:

A STRONG Woman's Guide to Retiring on Her Own Terms

ISBN: 9781072645467

Bookmark Editing, a division of J. Hill Marketing & Creative Services, Inc.
Cover design by Sooraj Mathew
Edited by Hilary Jastram and Kathryn DeHoyos
#pinkfix Productions

National #pinkfix Day!

◊◊◊

On May 17th, we invite you to join our #pinkfix Movement on National #pinkfix Day!

So, what does #pinkfix mean?

#pinkfix started in February of 2018 when we launched the NEW version of our blog Not Your Father's Advisor. We updated the old logo to our famous black and pink and added my Jessica Weaver logo also in black and pink. I kept using the term "get your pink fix" by referring to the website visitors who gained what they needed that day to help them move forward with their money and life.

#pinkfix has morphed into so much more than that. I started doing the #pinkfix for anything pink, for anything to do with our work, our community, and even my family...especially my Andie Girl! I became known as the pink advisor, always showing up in our pink with pink lips, pink STRONG bracelets, and all! People would reference me when they wore pink, "Oh, I'm just pulling a Jess Weaver." It became its own entity...the #pinkfix!

As I was journaling the other day about pinkfix, I wrote down words such as:

- Transformation, change, level up,
- Financial control, stability, confidence, security, freedom, stability
- Value, self-worth, net-worth
- Mindset, beliefs, behaviors
- Strong, confident, fabulous, courageous, inspiring, encouraging

Then I wrote down quickfix and put a HUGE X through it.

I crossed it out and wrote pinkfix. You see, a quick fix is what we are always looking for, but never ends up working for us. Society has been telling us that all we need is a quick fix. A quick fix is all we have time for! It is like a band-aid that works in the short term but isn't the REAL change we are looking for OR deserve.

It hit me!

People need a #pinkfix, and that what this is all about, making a lasting change/impact/transformation in your life that you deserve, and it all starts with your money.

For the widow, who just lost her husband and has no idea what to do with the money and how she'll be able to support herself. For the corporate employee, who wants to retire without the fear of running out of money and being a burden on her kids. For the new mom, trying to juggle work, kids, and managing the money without losing her sanity! For the woman sandwiched between caring for her parents while supporting her children, who feels her own life is slipping away.

#pinkfix is a life reset button, a reset to your money, to your mind, to your life, to your goals. It can be anything that helps you live your best life by pushing you out of your comfort zone. It raises the bar for your life and challenges you in a positive way. It can be one BIG thing OR lots of little things that add up to a bigger whole.

After reading this...do you need a #pinkfix in your life?

Most women think they need to figure out all their life questions first, BUT the women who have the most success know they need to take care of their money first so they can figure all the other stuff out with a sense of peace and security with their money.

Dedication

On the eve of two of my clients retiring, I thought it was fitting to write my book dedication. *Time to Refine* is dedicated to the first members of my Strong Retirement Club™. They all took a leap of faith and joined our community before it even existed! The Club has never been about me; it has always been about these incredible women, all fabulous in their own ways. I'm just there guiding them along in their transition into retirement. Yet, because of them, we have so much joy, love, and support. Their eagerness to learn, embrace new possibilities, and gain from this new experience, brings me to tears.

They get it!

They understand why it is so important to have a community around you as you make such BIG life decisions and stare retirement in the eyes.

Community, Confidence, and Control...that is what we are all about here at the Strong Retirement Club™. You are not alone in this; at least you don't have to be.

Thank you Georgann, Lan, Judy, Tina, Lori, Joanne, Kimberly, and Sandi!

Now, we get to welcome you into our community; we are grateful to have you here with us during our journey. I'm here to support you, just like I support my club members. My Strong Retirement Club™ was built for the women in the club, just like this book was built for you.

Always remember, the moment you feel alone, or feel the need to isolate yourself, is the moment to reach out. Embrace the women in your life who want to help; we are there for a reason because we care.

Table of Contents

Foreword

◊◊◊

For more than a decade, I have had the privilege of working with thousands of women traveling on their life's personal and professional journeys, as founder of my women's empowerment organization, B.I.G. (Believe Inspire Grow).

Along the way, I have met amazing women who have made it their mission to help women transform their lives. Jessica Weaver is one of these special people. As a vibrant member of B.I.G., Jessica dedicates endless hours inspiring women to put themselves first, focus on their personal life goals and offers them access to easy-to-use tools and strategies can help them fund the life they want to live.

Time to Refine is Jessica's latest gift for women. Jessica's thesis is that many women view retirement as a part of their future lives. Instead, she implores women to embrace the reality that they are always actively living in a retirement stage of life. Given time, we have tremendous opportunities to make smart choices that can pave a steady and consistent path for our lives, no matter what comes our way.

Unlike many wealth specialists, Jess is authentically on a mission to empower women, and she doesn't sugarcoat our complicated life experiences and challenges. She vulnerably shares her own life "secrets" as a busy wife and young mother who is sometimes "too hard on herself." She understands firsthand the roller coaster life so many of us experience. Despite our nearly twenty-year age difference, Jessica and I share many common beliefs and a unified passion to convince women that we are worth living a vibrant, healthy, and fulfilled life. One that is not fully dependent upon others' choices and decisions.

1

Women's lives are notably different from men. While we passionately embrace our role as the planet's nurturers, for our partners, our children and even our parents, we often neglect to take care of our own selves, emotionally, physically, spiritually and financially. It's time to choose a life of empowerment.

The dictionary definition of empowerment is "the process of becoming stronger and more confident, especially in controlling one's life and claiming one's rights." Jessica and I witness over and over again how women's complicated relationship with money often holds them back, rather than propel them forward. One fundamental realization we both share is that no woman can be truly empowered until she gains a solid understanding of her financial situation and embraces a willingness to make strategic plans specifically designed to fund her life's vision and her vision for the lives of the people she loves.

Now, we're not talking about who is bringing home the paycheck. There are many honorable reasons why women are not the primary breadwinner. We're talking about confidently exercising your voice about what happens to the family funds once they arrive in your bank accounts and financial portfolios. Despite the fact that women make 80% of all the consumer purchase decisions for our families, too many women "tune out" when it comes to long term planning. In order to have choices for your future life, you must "tune in" to your financial circumstances today.

Time is one of our greatest financial assets. Regardless of your current financial situation, one thing is certain - it will change! It can change for the better if you make a smart and dedicated plan and is likely to change for the worse if you do nothing .

Ladies, it's time to put on your "big girl pants" and stop making excuses for your financial avoidance. While there is no crystal ball that can predict all our future financial needs, "hoping" it will all work out is simply not a responsible option. It also keeps us from being the female role models our daughters and the young women of the next generation deserve.

At its very core, money is simply "fuel" for our goals and dreams. No fuel. No go. It's almost that simple. Managing It doesn't need to be an intimidating experience. Thanks to dedicated and compassionate financial educators like Jessica, this experience can actually be freeing.

Congratulate yourself for taking the first important step by choosing to read Time to Refine.

Knowledge is power. The women who consciously chose to become actively engaged in their financial lives discover an entirely new world. One where their voices are heard. One where their opinions are validated. And one where they are able to live the life they are meant to live.

Bravo for choosing to be an empowered woman.

- Tara McKenzie Gilvar
CEO & Founder, B.I.G. (Believe Inspire Grow)
A Women's Empowerment Organization

Introduction

◊◊◊

I had a defining moment in my life last year. A moment that shakes you to your core. One that changes your world forever reshapes your priorities and gives you a new perspective on life. I've been refining my life ever since, and I'd like to share with you how it began. In life, you have defining moments, and then you have refining moments that follow because you know your life can never be the same.

Throughout my journey, I've learned 3 REVELATIONS that are crucial to living on your own terms. Realizing these three epiphanies completely shifted my world, how I operate, and how I can NOW deliver the highest level to the women I work with. My hope is they will also shift your world, the way you think, and most importantly, the way you work your retirement. Because that is why you are here, to find out if you can retire on your own terms!

My insights began in the hospital when I was just shy of 36 weeks pregnant. I called my boss/father to tell him to rearrange my schedule for the next few weeks. "Why?" he asked. "Because I'm in labor, and I don't think I'll be making the meetings." I had scheduled several client meetings to squeeze in before my baby girl was to enter this world, but she had other plans. We should have known then what a determined little girl she was going to become!

I spent six weeks home with my baby, trying to figure out my new life as a mom...and as a working mom. Already the guilt had sunk in like other mothers feel. I kept thinking: *I should be doing work*. I would write blog posts, work on my marketing, and even kept a journal to fill in my never-ending cycle of ideas! I went back to work after the six weeks were up, which brought us to the holidays. I was feeling good, got some sleep most nights, and thought *I can do this*. By the New Year, I was jumping for joy at what the year would bring my family and career. Andie was settled at daycare with some fabulous teachers, and I was settling into this mom role...so I thought.

I began the year with four Retirement Roundtables, which are events for women near or in retirement that encourage them to talk about their fears and concerns around retirement. I hosted several other women's events, had numerous speaking engagements, began another mentorship with my business coach, and created my Strong Retirement Club™. I threw myself into work day after day. I lived on what must have been adrenaline!

And then it started, one Monday morning when I was on a call with my accountability buddy, you may have heard of her, Lisa Chastain. She is a rock star to put it lightly! Lisa is a Money Coach for millennial women out of Las Vegas, and we have partnered to bring even more value to our client's lives. In our partnership, we have weekly calls to discuss our actions for the week, our celebrations, what our higher standard will be, and lastly, we speak the truth. We have to tell each other one deep dark secret we are even afraid to admit to ourselves.

For several Mondays, I was only touching the surface of my secret. I didn't even know the magnitude of it until it hit me this one particular Monday, like an ocean wave crashing over you, leaving you breathless and in shock. Has that ever happened to you? All of a sudden, the BIGGEST issue you have been avoiding comes to light, and you are overwhelmed with a wave of emotions. By the end of it, you are exhausted yet also feel lighter. You feel there is finally hope for the first time in weeks, months, or years. I've experienced this in every one of my strategy sessions with a new woman client. Even though we don't have all the answers by the end of the session, they feel like they've found a new calm, a sense of relief, and new hope for their life and money. These women cry during our times together because they have been living with their secret for so long, they don't know how they got there. BUT in the end, they cry because they now see the light; they feel hope, and they are ready to move forward.

So, what was my secret I've been hiding from myself? I was dealing with postpartum depression and anxiety from having my amazing daughter, Andie. If I can pinpoint for how long, I would say for several months. I remember telling my husband months ago that I didn't want to celebrate any birthdays or holidays this year. He thought I was kidding and realizing how crazy my statement was I played along with him. But deep down, I was feeling too exhausted to celebrate anything and kept thinking what is the point of birthdays and holidays? Now, if you know me, you know how excited I get just over birthday cake! So obviously, this was not a normal comment for me.

Have you ever had an issue in your life where you felt like it was too difficult to deal with, so you keep yourself busy to distract yourself from it? What about with your money? Have you ever felt like it was too painful to take a good hard look at your money issues, so you distracted yourself with busy work? You research the topic to death, you ignore it completely, or you keep telling yourself *it isn't that bad.*

Well, you can guess what I did! I kept myself so busy my first year of being a mom. I created two programs, my Money Makeover program and my Strong Retirement Club™. I brought on over 20 new clients and did about three speaking engagements per month with over 10 of my own events and workshops. Looking back, I have no idea how I did it all. But again, I was trying to hide a big secret from myself, hoping my work would pull me out of a downward spiral I was dealing with mentally.

My first realization was there are times in our life when we keep ourselves so busy to distract from the real issue. We think it is more painful to deal with the issue, so we ignore it. Then we get into a pattern of feeling like we need to be busy to be productive each day, and if I only keep moving, then I MUST be moving forward in life. AND it hit me how wrong I've been. We can fill our days with so much busy work that we don't have a second to breathe, yet what did we really accomplish? Did you move forward with your goals or just add items to your to-do list to take up space.

So many women I work with and have met, admit the same thing. They avoid looking at their retirement because retirement scares them. They are terrified of running out of money and becoming a burden. They are nervous they will be bored at home, and their health will fail them. In the end, who will take care of me if I can no longer take care of myself? Will I fail myself if I plan it out all wrong such as forgetting to include the unexpected costs, missing a HUGE opportunity, or paying too much in taxes???

When this happens, we stay paralyzed, stuck in a waiting place, and too scared to find out the answers.

Are you stuck in the waiting place?

I was when I was hiding behind my secret until Lisa made me open up. It wasn't easy, I cried and trembled when I said it out loud for the first time. My husband was shocked; my family had no idea, and my friends couldn't believe it. They all thought I had it all together, all the time.

You see, we all wear masks. But it's time to take the masks off and be our authentic selves! Having Lisa there with me to figure out my secret and what my next step toward my recovery would be was crucial. I had to talk with my husband and open up because I knew he didn't want me hurting any longer, which brings me to my next realization.

There are times in our lives when the RIGHT people come into our world. My business coach Robyn Crane came into my life at the exact moment I needed her. If her LinkedIn message had come a year before or after, I would have quickly deleted it, but at that time, I knew I needed help. Robyn led me to Lisa, and Lisa and I became so close at the exact time when we needed each other. I was there to help Lisa through a really tough time, and she helped me in return. You need to embrace those people coming into your life just as I did with Robyn and Lisa. You are in my world for a reason; you are reading this book for a reason.

Ask yourself, what drew you to it and to me? What is the secret you've been hiding from?

Women come to me to get answers to quick questions. "How can I save more money for retirement?" "When should I take social security?" "How can I make an income from my savings?"

But all these questions hide your real concerns. *Will I have enough money to retire and not become a burden? What if I make the wrong decision and fail myself? How do I know if I have enough money to live on, so I won't have to eat dog food for the rest of my life? Do I have to stay at a job I HATE to save more money?*

Once the women decide to partner with me, I become their advocate and fight for what they want. It's so important for me to find the right women to work with because I personally take on their retirement goals and dreams. My commitment to you with this book is to be your advocate throughout it. I want to help you and serve you at my highest level. I have spent years studying about retirement, talking with women who are nearing or in retirement, and am obsessed with their fears and concerns. You have come into my life for a reason, and it is to transform your retirement into refinement, so you can retire on YOUR own terms!

Now, my last realization comes into play. I've come to an understanding in my life and the lives of the women I work with that we can have whatever it is we want, BUT we have to invest our time and money to have it. There is ALWAYS a tradeoff. You can't merely buy this book and think your retirement is all set. You need to invest your time and energy into reading it, into completing the tasks, and asking for help when you need it. I would be giving you false hope if I didn't say this! I had to invest my own time, money, and emotions to get better for my family's sake and for my own sake. I had to take time away from my family and work, which I did NOT want to do. But if I kept hiding from my secret, I wouldn't be helping anyone! I encourage you to stop hiding from your secrets and embrace them because we are going to BREAK through to what you need!

Are you ready to move past your secrets and your fears, and start this incredible journey with me? It's your life, so I ask you: Do you want to spend it hiding from your fears or live it up? Remember a strong woman looks a challenge in the eye and gives it a wink.

You, my friend, are a strong woman.

Time to Refine:

A STRONG Woman's Guide to Retiring on Her Own Terms

Chapter 1: Wonder Woman Genetics

◊◊◊

"I am a strong woman because a strong woman raised me."
~Unknown

I still remember the moment when my mother received a call about my grandmother from the director of her retirement community. My mom was sitting on the stairs. I was around the corner in the foyer anxiously waiting to hear what was going on. My grandmother was bipolar and loved to fake being sick to get attention.

Unfortunately, she also attempted suicide more than once while my mom was growing up. My mother was the one to find her a few of those times. My father kept saying she was faking it, but I KNEW this time was different. My mom was shaking, crying, and in shock. As she hung up the phone, all she could say was she needed to get to her mom.

Isn't it amazing how we always go back to viewing our mother as "mom" in times of crisis? It seems we never outgrow that instinct. I was seeing my mom with her own grown children—I was a senior in high school, and my brother was in college—yet she was viewing her mom as if she was a 5-year-old again.

"Mommy, please don't leave us!"

If you have ever felt your mom slipping away, or you lost your mom, did you feel that way?

My mom went into planning mode right after the call. She NEEDED to get to Florida from New Jersey fast. This was step one, so my father got on the phone and booked a flight immediately. NEXT, she had to get a hold of her brothers! Doesn't seem too hard, right? Well, one brother lived across the United States, BUT the other one lived in Malaysia. Third, she had to go through my schedule and my brother's schedule with my father since we both had sports commitments. Lastly, she wondered if she should bring a black dress or not.

My grandmother had a stroke. My cousin found her the next day lying in her bed, unresponsive. By the time they got to her, she was barely breathing. She was rushed to the hospital, but she had lost oxygen to her brain for a few minutes, which left her braindead. She was put on life support until my uncles could get there, and then the family made the final decision to take her off life support. We got the call the day before to tell us our Nana wasn't going to make it. My father, brother, and I boarded a plane and prepared for the next phase: her funeral. My mom had me pack her black dress to bring to her.

I still go through the events of those few days thinking there has to be more we could have done to prevent her death. *Did she need extra care? Was her health deteriorating more than we thought? How do we make sure it doesn't happen to more women living on their own later in life?*

The funeral was a celebration of the vivacious, feisty, and charming woman my grandmother was. If you don't know her story, read my first book *Strong Woman Stronger Assets*, where you will learn my grandmother went through two crazy divorces, her last one being from a man named Fred who was a cross-dressing alcoholic with two mistresses. She was a tough one, my grandmother, despite her constant battle with bipolar disease. We wanted to honor her the best way we could.

Then after the funeral issues started.

My mother and her two brothers all met with the estate attorney. You might have an idea where this is going...

My uncle immediately demanded that he take my grandmother's 12-year-old dog but would need $30,000 to go towards the dog's costs. The attorney couldn't stop laughing at this request. He must have also been terrified of what the nut would ask for next! This same uncle was gifted land in St. Thomas earlier in his life from my grandmother, which was his inheritance from her. Because of this gift, my grandmother left him a small inheritance in her will, which seemed to make sense to everyone but my uncle. He had multiple temper tantrums over his very small inheritance, called and yelled at my mother several times, and wouldn't let it go. As you can infer, he now doesn't talk to anyone in the family, and we ended up with my grandmother's dog.

The sad part is we haven't seen my cousin, his daughter since the funeral, over 12 years ago. Again, I thought, *there must be something we could have done to prevent these problems with the estate planning.* So many families are torn apart because there isn't an estate plan or as was the case with us, the plan wasn't discussed with the hotheads of the family.

My line of work proves that our family is just one example of how families can fall apart after a death.

By the last day in my grandmother's house, my uncle's wife had taken as many of my grandmother's possessions as she could fit in her luggage—especially the designer handbags and sunglasses. My mother's aunt made a guest appearance during our time in Florida, and she took much pleasure shopping in my grandmother's house as well. My grandmother and her sister hadn't spoken in over 30 years, yet my great aunt felt very entitled to her belongings.

AGAIN, there must have been something we could have done to prevent this!

I've been turning these thoughts over and over again in my mind trying to find a way to help women plan and prevent these tragic turns from happening.

AND it is happening! My neighbor just had a stroke. Her daughter, who lived with her, left for work one day and came home to find her mother barely responsive. The daughter was in shock for weeks after it happened. She felt so alone, overwhelmed, and lost. All the accounts were frozen, the pension money from her mom stopped coming in, the social security checks stopped being deposited, and she wondered how she would afford the house. Her income doesn't even cover the property taxes, let alone the maintenance and utilities. She's about to lose the house she has lived in for over 55 years in addition to losing her mother!

As she's trying to grieve the sudden passing of her mother she's worried about where she will live. Predicaments like these are what I've been dedicating the last several years of my life trying to fix. This book is a combination of that journey and the journey of the women in my Strong Retirement Club™.

My dedication to fixing this huge and increasing problem became a bit of an obsession.

I talked with numerous women who have gone through, are going through, or are scared these particular situations. What I found was amazing! The number one fear that women have as they grow older is becoming a burden. The next two fears go hand in hand with number one: losing their independence and running out of money. They are related because they result in becoming a burden. Next, I researched! I read over 10 books, lots of articles, and spoke with professionals who deal with retirees daily. Lastly, I hosted six Retirement Roundtables in one year. Needless to say, they became very popular and are still my number one workshop!

The Retirement Roundtable's only purpose was to dive deeper into women's fears. We centered on four topics: lifestyle, money, health, and estate planning. I'd ask the women participating: What are your questions, concerns, fears, and your own stories/insights in regard to each topic? I'd set my stopwatch for each topic, and we dove in! Every time, the women opened up more and more, they shared stories, asked questions, and brought up so many issues. I also invited several professionals to each roundtable, from Medicare consultants to estate attorneys, health coaches, bill payers, and so many more. They added so much to our conversations, and every woman left having gained a network of women professionals they can lean on in times of need.

Lastly, my Strong Retirement Club™ was born! It was my baby for the year! I knew there was a HUGE missing piece to the traditional financial planning, and it might not even be a piece that technically should be included, BUT I found a way to link the missing piece AND bring women together to reach their goals. To form bonds they never knew they could forge at this stage in their lives. The Strong Retirement Club™ complements what advisors are already doing for your retirement plan, allowing you to be more hands-on, and learn how every element all works together. I found this to be the most important piece; it revealed that women no longer felt they had control over their own money. Managing money was always done for them by their husband, father, or advisor. And even though the finances were being "handled," women were still being left in the dark.

Do you feel like you no longer have control over your own money?

Are you alone, scared, and overwhelmed? These women felt the same and were waiting for someone like me, who is so UNTRADITIONAL and UNCONVENTIONAL, to take a stand on what they needed for themselves and their lives. What they really needed was someone to breathe new life into them and re-energize them! Do you need an advocate for your life?

Join me in the pages of this book, where you will soon learn you are not alone.

The women who started in my club were ready to take a stance on this vital topic; they were eager to get control over their money and retirement. And it's so important to do this now. Why? Because if you have fears surrounding your money while you are working, imagine how much worse they will get when you no longer have that cushy paycheck? You have been brainwashed your entire life that you need a paycheck to survive. How else will you afford the roof over your head, the food on the table, the clothes on your back (or I prefer the stilettos on your feet!)? Well, in retirement, there is no paycheck; you have to create your own. Any financial issues you have now, only get intensified in retirement. Your financial insecurities get worse and worse, so let's take action now and start this incredible journey together!

Because this book in your hands was created from our Strong Retirement Club™, let's examine the creation of the club.

Three VITAL components were needed for the club to work and bring tremendous power to the women in it.

1. I wanted it to be a group of women who can bond and relate with one another because our strength is in our stories that we can share and learn from.

2. There needed to be knowledge. An education that not only I thought the women needed to hear, but of what they wanted to hear. I interviewed over 100 women, hosted Retirement Roundtables, and conducted surveys to find out the real fears around retirement.

3. The final ingredient is implementation. How can we implement the knowledge from the courses into our own lives? Knowledge is valuable, but if you don't know what to do with it, then it is useless. Throughout the book, I'll share with you different worksheets to help you implement the information and reflect back on it.

And so, the club was formed!

The club is an educational, inspiring, and communal group of women looking to take their retirement by the horns and actually ENJOY their happily ever after. I know, everyone says they will love being retired. But then the HUGE concerns, fears, and questions come up, and you live every day terrified. You're terrified of spending any money, terrified of not having a paycheck, terrified of your decreasing health, and terrified of outliving your money.

You've worked so hard the past 30-40 years for your retirement. It's time to start enjoying life.

In the club, you will be surrounded by a group of women who will encourage and empower you! We have the community of support, the tools to gain the confidence you need and desire, AND that will give you back the control over your retirement.

To give you a brief insight into how the book is designed, here is a summary of each topic that we will later dive into!

1. Properly Funding your Lifestyle: In this section, we will help you create the lifestyle in retirement you really want. You will learn how to create structure, live with a purpose, and feel fulfilled every day. We will teach you how you can lower your overall expenses, properly budget for your living costs and unexpected costs, do a dry run of your retirement, and other strategies to set yourself up for success.

2. Health and Long-Term Care: We will explore how to keep yourself in good health, the costs of healthcare during retirement, and different Long-Term Care planning strategies.

3. Building Your Retirement Plan: What does retirement look with all of your moving parts? Find out how it all works together and get a CLEAR view of every day. In this section, you will learn about: income, expenses, assets, inflation, social security, pension, taxes, Required Minimum Distributions (RMD), withdrawal percentage rates, and investment returns.

4. How to plan your legacy and validate your relationships with your loved ones. Whether you are considering children, charity, or loved

ones as you move forward, a proper plan will give you peace while making the most of your money. How to begin planning your estate, which documents you need, and how often you need to update them will all be covered.

At the start of the club, the women completed an assessment to determine where they stand now, where they should focus their year, and how they can improve their score. I've performed this assessment with every woman that comes into my world, and here is what I've found. About 90% of the women score 50% or below. They've done a great job getting themselves halfway. What I've learned from my own business and through the women I work with is that we can only get ourselves so far before we need to work or partner with someone to get us to the next level. I was able to get myself to a certain point before I hired my coach. You can get yourself on the right path with your savings and some investments before you need an advisor to filter through all your questions, and what you need to implement now, and later to get yourself to AND through retirement.

Next, go to www.jessicaweaver.com/moneybaggage and download the Financial Confidence Assessment. Take some time to go through it and be very honest with yourself. I'd love to hear your results so message me at strongwomanstrongerassets@gmail.com with them!

Pay attention as you go through the assessment to see which areas you've scored under a seven. Pay special attention to these areas as you read this book!

Wow, am I excited you are here with me now! Let's begin with my favorite activity that we do at the start of all my Retirement Roundtables!

Go buy yourself a retirement card. Once you get home, write on the envelope the date you want to retire. I'm not lying when I say one of the women in the club did this during the roundtable, and the next day; she told her boss that her last day would be 12/31/2018! How cool is that? She said doing this was the most impactful action she'd taken for her retirement. It made it REAL! After you write down the date, open up the card and write down the TOP three retirement dreams you have. Then seal the card back up in the envelope and put it somewhere safe. When the date on the envelope arrives, open the card and get to work on your dreams.

Create a plan to make your top dream a reality by the end of the year.

I did this exact thing when I was forming my Strong Retirement Club™; I put together a date for it to start, an action plan of how to fulfill it, identified who it was for, and what it would be comprised of. A retirement plan is very similar to a business plan. It goes beyond the financing, and into how you will make money, who you will serve, the costs, and where it will be located? In a related manner, you need to find your income sources, learn what your costs are, how you will live, and all the components that will make up your retirement. You can't go into building a business blindly, just like you can't go into building a retirement blindly.

Don't worry; we'll talk about it in the next chapter!

You definitely have the opportunity to join.

Chapter 2: Giving Birth to a Dream

◊◊◊

"She was powerful not because she wasn't scared but because she
on so strongly, despite the fear."
~Atticus

The night before my first live in-person event for my club, I had
a dream about giving birth. In the dream, I gave birth, but I
didn't have any pain which is strange since I gave birth a year ago
and can still remember the pain...before, during, and after. I
realized later what the dream was about; I was giving birth to my
Strong Retirement Club™. The gestation of my club took about as
long as my pregnancy with my daughter.

The conception of the club started when I noted a problem the
women I worked with were having. Then I noticed the problem
applied to women everywhere, near or in retirement, married or
single, wealthy or not. Next, I found the solution but had to create
and fine-tune the content to help these women. Lastly, I had to fill
the club with the RIGHT women. So yes, it did feel like giving birth!

To give you a taste of one of the most pivotal moments of the club,
here is an excerpt from my journal:

9/12/2018

Tonight is the first LIVE in-person event for the Strong Retirement
Club™. It is a stormy night, yet the women made it out because they
know how important it is to put retirement as a priority! I have
cameras ready to record all the goodies throughout the two-hour
event for the women not in attendance, but also for YOU. You are
now on our journey and will hear the stories of the women in the
room this night. The women coming from different backgrounds,
different careers, different family lives, all had one thing in
common. Retirement was looming over their heads in BIG ways.

One was terrified of how she would live on a limited income. Another was scared she wasn't optimizing her money enough. A woman already in retirement wanted to make sure she was doing everything she could to take care of her family now AND when she is no longer here. And the last woman was shaking in her high heels about how she would create a business in retirement to give back in even bigger ways than she had while she was working. A baker was trying to put together a plan to retire before her health forced her to while continuing to do what she loved. A teacher was juggling different major life decisions while wondering if retiring will set her back or move her forward. So many different questions, concerns, and thoughts ran rampant through their minds to a point when they wondered...*do I still have any control over my life*?

Retirement was looming over all of them but in different ways.

They came together as they joined my Strong Retirement Club™, mostly to learn more from me. But, my favorite part of the night was seeing how much they were learning from each other. Have you ever had a HUGE dream? A vision for your life, and then seen it come to life? This is exactly what happened on that stormy night; my vision for my work intensified to a shining ray of light. As I sat back and witnessed these women trading stories and insights, I noted they had a new eagerness to learn not only from me but from each other.

Getting the club up wasn't a seamless operation either. These women were all skeptical about using a club format for retirement planning. I had to sell them hard on the notion of how supportive it can be, how it would even be inspiring at times, and how the bonds that were formed would last a lifetime when the community is done right. And now, we are only two months in, and they are sold on it! Because they all bring something to the table we sit at, and now YOU bring something to the table. So, come on this journey with us as we go through a year of retirement planning in the most **non-traditional** way. I am Not Your Father's Advisor after all ;).

You are NOT afraid of retirement, just like these women are not afraid of retirement. You are afraid of what is in retirement. There are common fears and concerns among the women I'm working with in the club and among all the women I've interviewed for this book, and as I was creating my club. There is also insight that differentiates those fears and gives you a different perspective on them.

If your mom had Alzheimer's, for example, then you are more likely to be terrified of seeing what is happening to her happening to you. Similarly, another woman might still be scared of Alzheimer's even if she's never witnessed the reality of the disease.

You are scared because you KNOW what happens to an Alzheimer's patient, the other woman who has no experience with the disease is scared because she has NO idea what happens to an Alzheimer's patient.

The goal of the club is to identify your fears, concerns, and questions, and find solutions to move you past them. We have to get you past them, so they don't paralyze you from moving forward with a fulfilling retirement. Let's start with gaining clarity on your fears for retirement because remember; you aren't scared of retirement, you are scared of what's in it, and what it's comprised of.

Here are the common fears about retirement I hear about:

- Running out of money.
- Becoming a burden.
- Losing my independence.
- My declining health.
- The costs of my declining health.
- Having my financial affairs managed if my health declines.
- Being bored at home.
- Not utilizing my time so I feel fulfilled each day.
- Losing my purpose in life.
- Knowing my loved ones will be taken care of.

What are your top fears?

_____

_____

_____

_____

_____

_____

What do your fears stem from? Have you seen a parent or grandparent struggle with any of your fears? Have you had to support a loved one, whether financially or with their health? Maybe you don't have children or want your children to have to take care of you. I get it, they have their own lives, and when you are taking care of a loved one, you do put your life on hold. Maybe you don't want that for your kids? Have you heard stories that scare you? Have you not planned out what you need to do so you are scared of the unknown? If you don't know what retirement will look like, it will scare you!

Some of the women in the club are single without children, so they were terrified of running out of money and then what? One woman, in particular, we will call her Jane, left the corporate world to become a baker. She LOVES baking and even brings homemade desserts to every club meeting (a nice bonus!). She now wants to start her own little business so she can leave the horrible working hours of a bakery. Plus, her health doesn't allow her to maintain long hours anymore. *As you will learn, sometimes when we retire isn't up to us.* Sometimes, our health tells us we need to retire, our industry pushes us out, or we have to leave to take care of a loved one. It isn't always our choice, so being proactive as you are now is key! In Jane's case, she has been independent her entire life. She secured a good job in the corporate world, helped build a company, sold the company, and then was laid off. She decided to do something she loved versus what that was expected of her as a corporate employee. Jane went to culinary school, and I still remember sending her an apron on her graduation day.

Jane worked at several different bakeries, and she loved it. But as her life changed, her health changed, and she was ready for a change of work. The problem is that because she has been independent her entire adult life, the opposite of independence terrifies her! It's an unknown to her, she doesn't know how to be dependent on someone, and she's afraid to learn how. This fear rears its ugly head in various ways. Running out of money forces you to become dependent financially on someone else. Declining health makes you dependent as well. Struggling with memory loss will make you dependent on someone.

How do we get Jane past these scenarios so she can move on with her life and retirement? If we don't, she will stay at the bakery until her health gives out, and then she really won't be able to enjoy her retirement. That's what happens with these fears when they aren't addressed; they keep you stuck exactly where you are until something forces you out. Job loss, deteriorating health, industry changes, the list goes on and on. I don't want you forced out. I want you to go out on your OWN terms and in a big way! There is so much out there for you in retirement, so declare right now, it will be on your OWN terms. You decide when, where, and how.

What I learned our first night was about the missing components in traditional financial planning, and why they are failing you. Jane has been a client of ours for over 10 years. Even though we've shown her the retirement projection numerous times, she still had these looming fears. She still felt an uneasiness about her retirement.

Let's take a look at why she still had these fears despite the planning we've done. It comes down to 4 key reasons:

1. Because Jane didn't understand how the plan was built, all the assumptions, the components, and the data that went into the building of it, she didn't get it. The plan was over her head, just like it's over most people's heads (besides the advisors putting it

together). Not understanding your plan brings us to the next concern on the list. She didn't understand her plan because she didn't have the knowledge about how it works.

2. Because Jane didn't have knowledge of what goes into a plan, she didn't believe it. She didn't understand it and didn't know about the back work going into the plan, so she didn't believe the results. When we said she would have money at age 100, she said: "There is NO WAY that is true."

3. Because Jane didn't believe the results, it reinforced her fears and beliefs that she would run out of money. Running out of money was a very deep-rooted belief in her mind. What we believe is how we are going to act because our beliefs drive our emotions, which drive us to action.

4. Lastly, because Jane didn't believe in our plan, she didn't trust it. She didn't trust the results since they went against her ingrained belief/fear of running out of money. She didn't trust the plan, but truthfully, she really did not trust herself. The lack of understanding, the lack of knowledge, the lack of the right beliefs, all stemmed from a lack of trust in herself. If she ran out of money, what would that mean for her life? It meant she failed herself while also proving herself right about her belief that she would run out of money.

The overall theme of this book is to gain confidence and clarity in each of these components so you can live your best life in retirement. You'll read the information to gain the knowledge, hear stories to build your beliefs, and finally, find the trust in yourself that you can do it!

First, we will go through your lifestyle and money plan and learn how they merge together so you can create a comfortable plan to lean on and grow from.

Chapter 3: Rewriting Your Retirement into Refinement.

◊◊◊

"Nothing is more dangerous than a beautiful woman who is focused and unimpressed."
~Unknown

Doing research as I prepped to begin my Strong Retirement Club™ and create this book, I was so unimpressed with the information I encountered. The first perception I had to change was that retirement is the end of your life.

It's time to rewrite the script!

Retirement is NOT the end of your life; it is the beginning!

And you <u>have to plan</u> accordingly!

Your retirement takes a lifetime. You go from a working life to a living life once you make the shift toward retiring. Retirement, and for our purposes, Refinement, is divided into three KEY phases: the **Honeymoon**, the **Relaxation,** and the **Reflection**.

Do you know what will be involved in each phase for YOU?

The honeymoon is an exciting period just like when you fall in love for the first time! Every day becomes a Saturday, but this can be a benefit or bum you out. You can go nuts with activities and travel or sit at home twiddling your thumbs. There are three major components to this phase: your lifestyle, money, and health. Most advisors only focus on the money, but you and I know there's so much more to living a life of rewarding refinement than just the money, right?

How do we balance your lifestyle wants and needs with your budget? And how do we keep you healthy so you can enjoy what you want to do? Remember, you have worked so damn hard to get to where you are today! You've put off family time, trips, volunteering, and ME time to hustle your butt off and save. Now the time is coming, so how will you make the most of your honeymoon? If you're reading this, then I know you definitely don't want the traditional retirement! You don't want to sit at home and wait until your health gives out. That's not for you! You want to take retirement by the horns and live it, up baby! Learning how to structure your days is crucial to enjoying a fulfilling honeymoon! We will dive into building your retirement dream life by giving it structure, fulfillment, and a heavy dose of FUN later in this chapter!

Meet Kat!

Kat is a health and fitness coach out of Las Vegas, Nevada, who works with women over the age of 50, who are ready to take back control over their bodies and health. Kat is my pink soul sister and a fabulous woman. She is on this Earth to help women feel freaking fabulous in their skin and finally, live with confidence. Kat has been an active participant in our Strong Retirement Club™, joining us virtually to help women maintain their mobility, quality of life, and independence in retirement. Kat is also a #1 Best Selling author! Because our priorities shift, and health becomes a main focus in refinement, we wanted to include her in our book!

Here's an excerpt from my interview with Kat as it focuses on maintaining your health, independence, and mobility as long as you can in retirement!

Jess: Kat, explain who you typically work with and what their main problems are?

Kat: Typically, I work with women entrepreneurs or professionals like nurse practitioners, authors, small business entrepreneurs. Just motivated, driven women. Most of them are over the age of 50, and they are stressed out. They have put everyone before themselves. Their health might be declining, and they're ready to take control back in their life again and lose the excess weight. They are ready to get healthy and gain the confidence to love themselves and their lives.

Jess: Why is it that as women, we tend to always take care of everyone else before ourselves?

Kat: I believe that we perceive taking care of other people as selfless, and what we end up finding out to be truly selfless, we first have to make ourselves a priority, and in a sense, be selfish. Women just have a caring, giving nature; they always want to help and nurture, so inadvertently they start losing, or fail to create boundaries, and maintain what they need to be happy. Once they live their lives this way, they can't stop. It's part of their identity. "I'm a good person. I help people." But once they get into this cycle, then they start resenting the fact that they're not taking care of themselves.

Jess: I've seen family and friends, where there's an older couple, and the wife always takes care of the husband. The husband might have some medical issues, and then suddenly, because she's always taken care of her husband if she gets hurt, she passes away prematurely or before the husband. It's almost as though the whole time she was taking care of the husband; she wasn't feeling her best. But she didn't have the time or energy to take care of both her husband and herself. So, she picks her husband. I see with the older generation, especially. Women in their 80s and 90s have been taking care of everyone else so much that they don't make it to their check-ups at the doctors.

My husband's grandma always took care of her husband. She would actually clean the house every day. Not just once a week, every day. She would even pull out her oven to clean behind it every week. She was so busy, and she did everything for him. He had some issues, and they would go to the doctor, and the doctor actually looked at her one day and said, "You know what? I'm going to examine you. You don't seem that well." That's when they found cancer. From the time of her diagnosis to the time of her passing was only a few weeks.

This is a story that I hear a lot. It is so important to take care of ourselves, so we can keep taking care of everyone else.

Kat: Exactly. We see this type of scenario specifically with women, and then when we peel back those layers even more, we see it with women who are married, women who have families, women who are working in really big careers. Taking care of other people becomes part of their identity. What's important to note, is that helping others becomes so strongly ingrained in their identity that when that stops, they're left with themselves. Just as is the case when their husband passes away or they retire. Suddenly, they're alone and realizing, "Wow, I haven't taken care of myself. I haven't focused on me. What does that even look like? How do I even do that? Where do I begin?"

Before those big life events happen, they can start allocating 10 or 15 minutes a day to focusing on themselves and asking themselves, *what would make me feel good right now? What would impact my health, even in a small way right now?* Is it to take a 15-minute walk? To sign up with a trainer? To go grocery shopping and prepare food *I will enjoy, not just that my family will enjoy? What do I need to do this moment to make myself feel better*? Then just do it, instead of thinking of all the other reasons not to and why they should be focusing on other people or the house or this or that. Doing these other things is a distraction to taking care of themselves.

Jess: Exactly. They busy their days to distract from taking care of themselves.

Kat: We have to ask, "Why is that happening? Why are they putting themselves last? What's going on that this is their reality, and how did such a cycle even start? Where did they start putting themselves second? Where did they even begin?"

When women can identify when they became second-rate to themselves, they can understand why it happened and deal with the underlying issues, whether they are emotional, psychological, or relationship-based. Getting clear enables them to deal with where they went wrong so they can move forward into taking better care of themselves. But before they can put themselves first, healing is usually involved.

Jess: We do talk a lot in our retirement club and throughout this book about our identity. Our career might be our identity, or being a mother might be our identity. When we enter into retirement, usually those identities are gone, and we don't know what our purpose is anymore. As my mom says, she was forced into early retirement because she was mostly a stay-at-home mom, and then we grew up. There were no kids to take care of anymore. She felt very lost. That's a valuable perspective.

Kat: If you take off all the hats you wear, who are you beneath all the labels, titles, accomplishments, and failures, whether positive or negative? What is your identity? That's a really scary question to ask people because it's not usually tangible. It's not something we've ever really thought about. We've always thought, *I'm going to be a doctor. I'm going to be a manager*, etc. We don't think, *who do I want to be?*

Jess: Yes, before you're a mother, before you're a wife, an advisor or fitness coach, before all the things, the first thing you are is a woman. So, who are you as a woman? What do you do? You really need to do something each day to remind yourself of the type of woman you are and want to be. Obviously, health is a big part of that. What type of person do I want to be? Do I want to be exhausted all the time, uncomfortable in her own skin, or not confident anymore? Who are we? And what do we want to be?

What do you see people fear about their health as they age? You work with women in their 50s. In the back of their mind, they're probably thinking *if I don't get healthy now, when will I?*

Kat: Some women think I want to play with my grandchildren and not be stuck in a wheelchair on oxygen, or unable to walk. Or maybe they're thinking; I have so much more I want to see of the world. I want to go to Machu Picchu and actually hike it. I want to go to the Great Wall of China. I don't want to be stuck in a wheelchair or stuck on a cruise ship, just looking at the scenery. I want to actively participate in my life. What do we need to do these activities? We need mobility and strength, so we can stay independent and enjoy more years of our lives.

If these women are 50 and just now looking at their life, and let's say they're 100 pounds overweight, they're probably also asking themselves, *what's my family history? My mom died of a heart attack. My dad died of a heart attack. When am I going to die? Is it soon? Am I ready for that?* These are really tough questions to ask yourself, but they're so important. Maybe someone's actually relatively healthy, and they've been thin most of their life, but when they hit menopause, their body changes. Now, they have excess weight and body fat, and they can't figure out what to do. These changes, if they don't prepare for them, ruining their emotional relationship with themselves and their body image. They don't like the way they look anymore. They isolate themselves. They don't want to go out to public social events. They say no to movies and lunches with friends. They don't date.

Dating brings up another point. Very often, in the middle of our lives, women lose a husband or divorce. They want love again, but due to their health and physical body, they don't feel like they are worth it. Because who would love them at this weight, or looking like this? Who would love them if they haven't taken care of themselves?

Women face so many different scenarios in their 50s, but they can also confront these events at 30. Someone could be morbidly obese when they are younger; you don't have to wait for menopause. Their body can change after a traumatic life event or injury. All of a sudden, they're 60, and they've never had to worry about their weight or their health before, but now they have to. Where do you go from there?

Jess: And this issue probably brings us back to finding their identity. They might distract themselves from their new reality or try to ignore it.

Kat: I hear a lot of excuses. like, "I don't have time. I'm too tired. I don't feel good. I don't have the money. The gym's too expensive. I have other priorities." Excuses come up because it's easier to focus on other areas than it is to focus on ourselves.

It's like holding a mirror up to ourselves and asking honestly what is really going on?

It's easier to brush 20 pounds under the rug. *I'm totally happy, but I hate the way I look. I don't want to have sex with the lights on. I don't want to date. I hate wearing clothes. I hate going clothes shopping.* If those are your responses, are you totally happy? Or are you justifying what you are doing because for whatever reason it feels too scary to try to change it?

Jess: You're so right. As one woman in my club says, "If you don't make the time today, when will you?"

Kat: Anyone who has struggled with weight if they've lost weight and gained it back and yo-yoed 20 pounds or 100 pounds, psychologically, it sets you up for avoidance. You don't want to try to get a handle on your weight again. Why? Because you feel like you will fail. Why would we want to work toward a goal if we felt like we would just fail ultimately?
Jess: You have that scar.

Kat: Exactly. We want to avoid what causes us pain. You might hear a woman say she thinks of herself like: *I am a highly achieving woman. I have a doctorate in nurse practitioning. I bought my own house at this age. I've done all these amazing things. I help all these amazing people. But in my life, I still feel like a failure because I can't lose the weight and keep it off.* That's a disconnect in their life.

Jess: Part of your program is having your clients build up on little successes to find the right way to move forward in their lives. If there is a setback, how do you keep them focused on continuing to go ahead instead of falling off? That's what I see people with their money, and what I see people in retirement do with their health. When they try to do it on their own and are 100% committed to getting healthy or saving money, they might be able to get themselves halfway. But when the unexpected happens with their money or health, or they have an unanticipated expense or tough year, breakup or divorce, and they fall off, it's so much harder to get back on board and committed again.

Kat: That brings me to another topic. In many areas of our life, when we want to learn something new, what do we do? We go to school. And we find a support system there. Someone is teaching us and guiding us. We have our classmates or our virtual classmates. Others hold us accountable and are supportive of us in our journey, relating to the struggles we're going through. They cheer us on when we have victories. We have that support.

In my experience, a journey to losing weight or building more muscle, anything health-related, is often an isolated journey.

Women try to do it on their own and wonder why they aren't successful. It's because we need people surrounding us and supporting us. We need a guide to help us figure out the right actions to take. Women and men want a quick fix. They don't want to deal with the underlying problems, like why they got this way in the first place. They want a magic pill. They want a quick fix, a diet, a speedy exercise program. But what do all these things do? They teach them that they are failures. Because they lose weight and they gain it back. It's not that the women or men are failures. They are not failures. You are not a failure. You have just not been taking the right actions to get the results you truly want.

Jess: These "quick fixes" do them a disservice, as you said. As humans, we aren't built to do life on our own. We aren't built to know exactly what to do and when to do it. We're built to be connected and help one another.

Kat: Exactly. Taking these shortcuts doesn't teach you the skills to live your life. It doesn't teach you the skills to have a beautiful relationship with food. It doesn't teach you how to have a beautiful relationship with exercise, one that fits into your life and works with your life.

After discussing how to stay healthy and fit so you can enjoy your retirement, let's see what other stages are in store for you!

Relaxation Phase of Refinement

During relaxation, you'll slow down. You'll travel, and hang out with the grandkids, and volunteer. In short: you will simply enjoy your downtime. Staying social is key to keep your mind sharp and engaged. As you move through retirement, your friends from work will slowly drift away, and you'll need new friends to relate to. Community will be very important! Georgi, a member of my Strong Retirement Club™, gasped when she heard about the relaxation phase. She exclaimed that she couldn't wait to get there! Georgi has been retired for a few years and loves her life, but because she's retired, feels the need to help her family all the time. Her children live far away, (and by far, I mean a 45-minute drive on top of a 7-hour plan ride). When she's needed, she makes sure she's right there but doing this tires her out so much. When she envisions the coming years, the relaxation phase seems marvelous.

Reflection Phase of Refinement

Reflection is the time to look back on all you've accomplished and to figure how you can make an impact in the world It's a fascinating period because you will go from thinking about you to thinking about everyone else. As yourself: *what significance has your life had so far? How have I impacted the people around me?* Leaving a legacy and what that even looks like in your life will be on your mind more.

How cool would it be to leave an impact on this world that's even bigger when you are gone than the impact you had while you were here? When you start thinking that way, death won't scare you anymore. Traditional estate planning won't suit you because you're thinking even bigger now and can use someone who isn't your father's advisor to help you! My goal for you is to leave this world with no regrets, so you know you've lived your best life. And what better way of accomplishing this, than by committing to it now! Let's find a better way to live out your life and leave a legacy to this world that lasts the test of time.

You need all these components to live the nontraditional retirement, or as we call it refinement, and that is why I created my Strong Retirement Club™! To bring together a community of women, who have the same vision for themselves: to have an awesome retirement, make an impact, and leave a legacy! Your life doesn't end at retirement, at least it doesn't have to!

One of my favorite things about my club is that we allocate quarterly ME time when we gather together online for motivation and education! Each ME time is followed by an in-person exclusive club EVENT to learn how to instill the motivation and education you need for this phase of. To continue building the community, we hold annual wine tastings each year so you can meet women in all the retirement clubs and share your stories, and growth as you learn even more from one another.

Now that you understand all the stages of retirement, let's look at how you want to live during each phase. We'll start simply when examining how you want to live. Note that I said "simple," NOT "easy." While "How do you want to live" is a very simple and straightforward question, it can take you months, if not years to fully answer it.

That said, let me ask you: **How do you want to live?**

I recently returned from vacation with my family, which was amazing, but by the end of the week, I couldn't wait to get back into my routine. I LOVE my routine, or maybe it is more about how much I love a routine and what it does for my life. I love knowing when I'm going to work out when I'm going to eat (I'm a big grazer!) when I will drop my daughter off at school and pick her up. I just LOVE the knowing exactly what I'm going to do and when.

Have you ever felt this way toward the end of a vacation? *I can't wait to go back on my diet! I can't wait to start back at the gym! I can't wait to start saving money again and stop spending it*!

Humans are creatures of habit, and when we don't have structure, bad habits evolve quickly.

If you didn't work out yesterday, and figure you're on vacation so why work out today, you've started the snowball effect? Or maybe you can relate to this reasoning? *I've already spent $50 on ice cream for the kids, so what's another $300 for a lobster dinner*? That snowball gets bigger and bigger.

So, what happens if your new life in retirement turns into one VERY long vacation? You start to only wear sweatpants all day, then you stop showering most days, and then you become the cat lady who never leaves the house making your family genuinely concerned about you! This scenario might seem extreme, but you can see if it a short leap from refinement to crazy cat lady if you don't plan out your days in retirement.

What you lacked before has now become your biggest commodity: TIME! You have your time back, after so many years of working day in and day out, you finally can dictate how to you live your days. You only have to answer to yourself. Sounds great right? Well, it can be if you use your time wisely. When we don't schedule out our days, we become experts at procrastinating! Suddenly, you have an abundance of tomorrows. "Tomorrow, I'll go to the grocery store." Then: "Whoops! Didn't make it there today, so I'll go tomorrow." And then the next tomorrow. Now your milk is spoiled, and your husband is yelling there is no food in the house! I've heard from numerous women in retirement that one errand can take them all day. Once you have plenty of time in your bank account, you lose your efficiency with it!

I'm in the opposite arena with time!

I'm a new mom, and my daughter is celebrating her one-year birthday next week. When I have a full hour to get stuff done, I'm a tornado! It's amazing how efficient I have become (or hope I am!) with my time and getting tasks accomplished. They might not be done to perfection, but honestly, what mom has everything done perfectly? If it's done at all, I call *that* perfection! But as you are about to join this fun camp, I'm going to let you in on some secrets our retired women have shared. Shhh! Don't tell them the secret is out!

Actual retired women's go-to rules for getting stuff done in retirement!

1. Get one task accomplished each day.
2. Stay social with your daily engagements.
3. Always use and challenge your brain.
4. Find something every week to feel fulfilled in your life.
5. Stay away from people who waste your time! This has become my favorite tip and can be used by any person at any stage of life.

Now, we are going to dive into each of these secrets and explore how they can work for you.

One of the happiest retirees we work with is Linda, is the queen of what I call the Engagement Calendar! She is always off on another trip, volunteering to drive a friend down to Florida, to babysit her grandchildren, or doing group walks, and she basically lives on the go! She went through some very tough times, had a terrible divorce, rebuilt her new life, and then realized she just wants to have fun. Gaining clarity over what you want in retirement is the first step toward building your lifestyle. Go through this exercise to gain focus on how you want to live each day in retirement.

Retirement:

Describe an ideal day post-retirement.

You:

Your spouse:

Describe an ideal week post-retirement.

You:

Your spouse:

Describe an ideal month post-retirement.

You:

Your spouse:

Describe an ideal year post-retirement.
You:

Your spouse:

According to the book, *You Can Retire Sooner Than You Think*, by Wes Moss, happy retirees have three core pursuits. A core pursuit is an activity, engagement, exercise, hobby, or even simply something of interest to you. These core pursuits don't just show up at your door once you retire. You need to nourish them while you are working so you will have something to retire to, NOT something you are retiring from. Most people are too busy to find out what they enjoy doing, so they end up retiring from their job with nothing to retire to. This won't be you since you are reading my book! If you have no idea, start journaling. You can do this on your notepad, phone, or even on Post-its. Write down the times of day you feel pure joy, satisfaction, fulfillment, or as if you're being positively challenged. Take notice of the recurring times, activities, and such that bring these emotions. Then add more of them to your life and before you know it, you have a NEW core pursuit! My Strong Retirement Club™ has become a core pursuit in itself; the women meet regularly and educate themselves. They create bonds as they stay social and challenge themselves in ways that feel good. If you are short on core pursuits, schedule a Discovery Call to see if the club is a good fit for you at https://jessicaweaver.setmore.com/!

Here is my special equation to creating a productive engagement calendar without overcommitting your time. Because you didn't work so hard in your career to only work harder once you retire! To help add structure to your life, do one of the following items every day:

1. Work around the house.
2. Complete an ordinary errand.
3. Take part in a community activity to be social and engaged.
4. Spend time on a hobby that makes you smile.
5. Work on an activity that brings you personal enrichment. You can use my example of building the Strong Retirement Club™ to inspire your own ideas!

The greatest common denominator of an engagement calendar is being social. The number one core pursuit of unhappy retirees, according to Wes Moss and his survey, is reading. Why? Because it isn't social...unless you start a book club! Being social engages your mind, gets you out of your house, provides support and encouragement, and is a way to stay connected to society. Take our client Linda, who is always helping other women who are sick, need some company, or just want to liven up their existences. When you are social and helping others, it gives you purpose, and when you ask for help, you give someone else purpose. It is one of the best gifts you can give and receive: PURPOSE in life! It is why such an integral part of our human design is connection. We accomplish connection by being social and asking for or giving help.

Linda was always so upbeat when we spoke; she came to most of my events, and always responded right away to my calls. But then I noticed she was responding less and less, or she was taking more time than usual to get back to me. She was down whenever we spoke, so I knew something was wrong. Linda came in to meet with us in person so we could get a better idea of how she was really doing in her retirement. That's when we found out Linda was having trouble with her knee and was going to need surgery. She couldn't go on group walks around her neighborhood or attend her various social engagements because the pain was too much. She wasn't traveling at all.

Linda's world completely shifted and threw her into a depression. She wasn't as social, engaged, or connected, and she suffered because of that. Her memory started to go; her moods were off, and she withdrew more and more. She felt alone. The more alone she felt, the more she withdrew. According to Dr. Caroline Leaf in her book *Think, Learn, Succeed* isolation during times of stress and crisis can be deadlier than obesity. When Linda felt alone, it made her feel isolated and brought on a depression that delayed her recovery and well-being.

A few months after her knee surgery, she got back to her old self. Surprisingly, her memory was back, too. She was social again and taking part in her walking routine, as happy as ever. Most importantly, she was thankful. She was so appreciative that we made an effort to make sure she was fine, and that our team had gotten the necessary documents in place, in case she couldn't rebound. Making these plans gave her a HUGE sense of peace. She had a team around her to take care of her health, money, and life. It meant the world to her to have that peace.

Linda is proof we need to be social, engaged, and connected during retirement.

What will be your core pursuits?

How will you live your life in retirement while having a community around you?

You can find anything to enrich your time online nowadays, such as clubs, meetups, and activities. Roadscholar.org is a website for retirees, and seniorjobbank.org is a super resource to find jobs in retirement. You can start your own business, take college courses, or embark on a passion project. Some of the women in the club want to leave their career to start a new one that will give them both flexibility and satisfaction. If you are on track for a more career-oriented retirement, brainstorm on how your current work skillset can help you now.

There are so many options, here are a few to get you started!

- Venture capitalist clubs to help fund startup companies.
- SCORE signifies Service Corps of Retired Executives to help local businesses.
- Financial experts can help run the books for non-profits.
- Investment Clubs (yes, they still exist!) are a great way to better understand investments and markets.
- Habitat for Humanity.
- Tutoring, teaching at a local community college.
- Volunteer, consult, or work part-time.

But if you are shouting in your head, *I want to start my own thing*! Then let's go through the list of what you need to know. I'm a big fan of lists, which is why I have so many Post-its all over my notebooks, computers, and desks! You will become a big fan, too, after this exercise. Get your notebooks out, strong woman, it's time to write!

Create a list for each of the following:

1. Your interests, what gets your blood running?
2. Your skills.
3. Your ideas.
4. Clientele you'd like to work with and help. It's your business now, so you don't have to work with people who only bring you down!

5. Connections you can use to network with.

Next, have a plan B for your business. Maybe you aspired or built a business or endeavor that was too grand the first time around, and you don't that headache anymore! Do you remember Jane? She left the corporate world to become a baker. She's worked at a few different bakeries, but always had the dream of owning her own bakery. I thought that was such a cool aspiration! (Side note: I'd definitely gain 20 pounds if that were me!). Anyway, since she kept talking about it, we went through her retirement plan to see if she could manage to own a bakery with her money, and it turns out she could!

Still, as time went on, she kept hesitating on making the big decision to open her doors.

After about two years of all talk and no movement forward, I called her out on it. I asked her if deep down, she really wanted her own bakery. Because honestly, who wants to wake up at 3 a.m. every morning to run a bakery in retirement? Not many! And she admitted that probably no, she didn't want to take on such a BIG project, but maybe selling her goods at different stores and markets would be enough. This became her plan B, and a way to get her moving toward her goals instead of staying paralyzed at her current job. So, don't worry, you can have a plan B and be OK!

Lastly, it is important to understand that it costs money to start a business, and it takes a LOT of sweat equity. Think about how much time and money you are willing to invest in your idea. Consider how much support you will get from others, and not financially, but emotionally. It takes a ton of courage, reinforcements, and inspiration to start a business, and you need to know who is on your team or not.

Whether you will be building a new business, focusing your time on a passion project, volunteering, or traveling the world, there is a KEY component to everything we have talked about...expectations! You need to set the expectations you will have with yourself and your family. You don't want to be upset with your spouse every day because they want to sit at home and read the newspaper while you are off being a social butterfly! One woman in my retirement club said it took her a year to get over her husband not wanting to do any of her activities. She confessed she'd drive over his newspaper on purpose to get her frustration out! The problem wasn't her husband's view on what retirement should be versus her own view; it was her expectation that he would accompany her to everything. She couldn't wait for him to retire so she could share all her fun engagements with him!

Unfortunately, he had other plans that consisted of a couch and a newspaper (might have been a bit wrinkled after her assault on it!). Because of her high hopes, she was let down, and I don't want that to happen to you! She had to accept the fact that his refinement was not going to be the same as hers. Once she accepted it, she found other girlfriends to go along with her to all the events on her social calendar. Here's what I've witnessed and learned, so please, take notes!

You have to be very upfront about your expectations and be willing to try to understand your spouses and your family's mindsets. I did say TRY to understand, meaning, at the very least, go into the discussion with an open mind.

Expectation Talking Points:

1. Talk with your family (parents, children, siblings, etc.) about how much financial support you will give them. Give them a time frame on when support will be given! Too many baby boomers are still supporting their children while also taking care of their parents. They are sandwiched between two generations! Don't even get me started when they are changing both their kid's diapers and parent's diapers! Do what you can to prevent this situation.

2. Explain to your family how much physical support and time you will offer them. This includes driving to and from doctor's appointments, cleaning houses, bringing them food, and other gestures. They shouldn't expect you to take over everything now that you are retired just like you wouldn't expect them to do everything if they were retired. You MUST crush that expectation before it starts by openly

discussing this with your family. If only one person does all the caretaking, they will get resentful of their siblings, and that is when families fall apart. This also goes for babysitting the grandchildren. I have a one-year-old, and it is EXHAUSTING to watch her all day! Know your limits on babysitting and only offer what you can manage.

3. Family visits: when, how often, and how LONG! If you move away from your family, what are the guidelines for visiting you and for you to come back to stay with family members? By the way, who pays for these trips?

4. If you want to create a new business or hobby, how supportive will your family be? If you expect them to be your first customers, be at every art show, and so on, then you might be let down. They might not view your new initiative as a "true" business, as it should be! Have an open conversation to discover how encouraging they will be and what you will need from them as you start your new journey.

5. Finally, if you are married, be very open with what type of retirement you are after! Will it be low key and relaxing, or high energy and crushing your bucket list of activities? If you want to retire sooner than your spouse, will you take over more of the household tasks? If you work longer than your spouse, will he? Will you be more willing to take time off to travel or to do more activities during the workweek? Finally, remember to always talk numbers! Be explicit about how much to spend on trips versus other expenses.

Expectations come into play whether we are talking about family obligations, finances, lifestyle, and even legacy planning. I can't tell you how many couples have come into the office with the conflict that one of them wants to leave the children a ton of money in their estate while the other spouse wants to leave them nothing. Navigating retirement is about communicating expectations, so you both have a better understanding of where the other is coming from.

I've seen firsthand how differences in expectations can ruin relationships, business arrangements, and families.

If you have a certain expectation in mind, the other person might not know about it, or they might have a different plan in mind. I've learned the hard way that it isn't your obligation to live up to someone else's expectations just like it isn't their job to live up to your expectations. This is especially true when you don't communicate about both of your expectations!

Being the only female advisor at my office, and a new mom taught me a lot about expectations. The male way of working from 8 a.m. to 5 p.m. every day wasn't working for me, yet those were the expectations. My industry also tends to be very slow to progress with the times (to put it nicely), and the firm's expectations of very little innovation didn't work with my vision! I've been rewriting the script ever since I started the Women's Division of my firm years ago, but I had always struggled with the guilt. I felt guilty I couldn't live according to everyone else's terms. It ate me up inside! With the help of good friends, family, and a therapist, I can now see clearly that it isn't my job to live how everyone lives. I needed to find my own path forward to escape the anxiety, guilt, and depression I was putting on myself.

I now start every new relationship on the basis of what is expected of me and what is expected of the other party. Doing this levels the playing field and allows both of us to understand what type of relationship it will be, and what the goals and boundaries are. Having these types of conversation can be tough, but open communication is the only way forward! If you feel like you're living someone else's life, you may still be living according to someone else's expectations. If this is the case, it is even more important to complete the exercises to determine how YOU want to live your life, NOT how other people want you to live! Remember you are living on your own terms now!

Next up is finding a way to finance your new and refined life in retirement.

I call it finding your happy place! So, let's move onto the next chapter concerning colliding your lifestyle with your money and finding your happy place.

After all, there is no better place to be.

To begin your "Happy Place," take a moment to reflect on your current place in life. More specifically, what is working in your life and what is not working.

What is working:

What is not working:

There are reasons you are still attached to doing things that are no longer working for your life. It could be a fear that is holding you back or a moment in your past you still aren't over.

Journal the moments in your past, you are still holding onto, that you can't seem to let go of. Use these questions to guide your reflection.

- What are your emotions around it?
- How does it make you feel to stay stuck in your life because of this moment?
- Are you ready to forgive it and move forward?
- What has to happen to be able to forgive the moment or to forgive the person?

It's time to let go of the past, forgive it, and remove the areas in your life that aren't working. Focus on what is working and add to it. That is where you want to live in your refinement!

Now you are in the right mindset for the next chapter. Let's dive in!

Chapter 4: You Deserve More Than Status-Quo Retirement

◊◊◊

"Spoil me with loyalty, I can finance myself!"
~Unknown

We are ready to move onto your "happy place" where your lifestyle and money collide, in all the right ways! Since most people focus solely on the money aspect of retirement, I like to ask them how they want to live their numerous days in retirement...and they have no idea. Their answer is: "I've only been planning the money part of the equation."

Well if you don't know how you are going to spend your days, then how do you know how much you are going to spend?

If every day is a Saturday in retirement, which is the common saying, then you might get bored. And what happens when we are bored? We spend money! At least, I do; my husband can attest to that!

The other half of people I meet with only plan out their lifestyle.

Well if you don't know how much money you have to spend, how do you know what lifestyle you can afford?

Most people don't pay close attention to their spending, and as they earn more, they spend more. It's a cycle of earn more, spend more, earn even more, and spend even more. Then you get to retirement, and all of a sudden are expected to be on a budget.

That does NOT work!

It also doesn't work to spend without a plan because you will run out of money.

One woman I met with actually told me she will walk out into the ocean the day she runs out of money. I asked her, "What will happen if your health is amazing, and you have grandbabies, BUT you have no more money? Will you still walk out into the ocean?"

That question, thankfully, got through to her!

The happy place or sweet spot is where you learn how to balance both your lifestyle and money.

Lifestyle + Money = Happiness

We will add another variable to the equation soon enough...Health!

Now, it's time to talk about money and lifestyle. As you get closer to retirement, you want to lower your expenses as much as possible. This is one of the best actions you can take because the less money you spend on day-to-day expenses, the more money there is for the fun stuff. You want to have fun, and you even need to have fun after all the work you've put into your career.

The first step in the equation is lifestyle. It's time to bust out the calculator and take a good look at how much your life is costing you. Write down your expenses; circle the ones you won't have in retirement anymore and write down the new ones that will be added in retirement such as healthcare costs, additional travel, and hobbies. What is the total number?

The second step is money! List all forms of your income such as pension, social security, rental income, part-time work/consulting income, income from retirement accounts, income from non-retirement accounts, and so on.

You can build your retirement income with the help of our Strong Retirement Club™ worksheet!

Download it at:
https://www.strongretirementclub.com/free-workbook.

But how do you realize your income from your investments?

To do so, we have to make a few assumptions! We need to look at your asset size, the rate of return, and the withdrawal rate. It'll be easier if we look at an example!

Let's say...

You have $500,000 in your 401(k), and you want to withdraw $20,000 each year or 4% of the total account value. Your 401(k) also goes up by 8% that year (wow awesome job), which is $40,000.

$500,000 - $20,000 + $40,000= $520,000

High five! Your account went up even though you took money out! Woohoo! Let's repeat this cycle every year, and you'll be good to go. BUT hold on! We all know we can't always earn 8% each year AND you might need to withdraw more some years.

Now, let's say the next year, you call me and exclaim you have exciting news to share. You are taking the entire family on a trip to Italy! (Can I come???) You need to withdraw extra money, about $41,600 or 8% of your account value of $520,000. Unfortunately, it was also a poor year in the markets, so you only earn 2% on your account or $10,400. You're withdrawing $41,600 and only earn $10,400, so you have to tap into some principle, and by the end of the year, your account is $488,800.

Decreasing the principle is fine for a year or so, but if you are consistently taking more money out than you are adding, you will fall short and be living with your kids. Okay, maybe not, but you do need to watch that balance every year. This is why so many retired people work with an advisor. They don't want the burden of whether they will run out of money or not to fall entirely on them.

The third step is to see where you stand. Tally up all your income sources, subtract your expenses, and what is the number? Is it positive or negative?

Income - Expenses = Surplus or Deficit

If you have a surplus, another high five! Sorry, my daughter loves them; she'll give you 20 in a row!

If you have a deficit, let's keep going to balance out both pieces of the equation. We can raise your income, lower your expenses, or both!

How can you lower your expenses now? There are so many ways, and you just have to think outside the box and get creative!

I'm reminded of a club member who did a marvelous job of lowering her expenses while reducing her stress...money stress! So many times, we believe that selling a big house, getting rid of a car, or vacation house means we failed. But before you declare that you failed, let's revisit our beliefs: did the big house define who you are as a person? No! Did the vacation house define your success? No! Did the extra car show people who you really are? No! Julie, who is a rock star member of my first Strong Retirement Club (https://www.strongretirementclub.com/), ™ realized the material things she was surrounding herself with didn't define who she was and that they were only adding to her money stress. First, she had to gain clarity over what defined her life, and what made her happy and fulfilled. She came to find out it wasn't all those material items; what she really wanted was to retire without worrying about the money every day. She wanted to travel and spend time with her family. It wasn't a failure to get rid of those items; it would have been a failure to *keep them and put her retirement in jeopardy.*

Don't think retirement means you failed at working. Don't even fathom that selling and downsizing means you aren't rich enough! What it truly means is that you are finding your true self and telling society those things don't matter. To me, that is success! Knowing what will bring you happiness and satisfaction is success and is a KEY to living an authentic life. Once you identify what makes you happy, we need to find out how can we translate your money habits to correlate with living your most authentic life.

These are examples of how other women in the club reduced their expenses, and made their life simpler, YET more fulfilling!

- Pay off your house. A few precautions before you take your lump sum money and pay off your house: I wouldn't recommend using pre-tax retirement money to pay off your house. I also wouldn't suggest using anything more than 25% of your non-retirement (already taxed money such as your bank account or money market) to pay off your house. My favorite two strategies are to add an additional few hundred dollars to each mortgage payment towards your principal and to remit bi-weekly payments.

- Downsize your house, move to a cheaper state or rent. I live in New Jersey, and property taxes are very high. Our real estate is expensive; our utilities are pricey, and pretty much anything you buy in New Jersey is costly! It's hard to argue the benefits to stay in such an expensive state besides being close to family. But remember you are retired so you can travel home whenever you want. You aren't tied down by vacation days and sick days from your corporate job. When people leave New Jersey, they save on average $5,000-$10,000 in property taxes alone, which becomes their newfound travel budget. Yay! Wouldn't you rather spend that money on fun stuff than send it to the state each year?

- Buy a car while you are still working and pay it off. Yes, you will need to get another car some point in retirement but pay this one off first.

- Finish home renovations before retirement. It is much easier to pay for them when you have an income coming in versus taking too much from your nest egg to afford it. If you do need to do some renovating while you are retired, do it after a really good year of investment returns!

- Have a plan B! Think about another plan for retirement that will still make you happy and satisfied but will cost a whole lot less. If you want to be on the beach, can you move into a condo or be close to the beach and still be happy? Can you downsize your house so you can travel more? What does your plan B look like?

What about the other variable: Income? How can I raise my income to cover my living expenses?

Here are some creative ways to increase your income besides getting a part-time job or consulting gigs!

- Rent out rooms in your house through Airbnb; I know several people who have done it!
- House sitting, dog sitting! Our dog walker retired from the retail world and now LOVES her job. She gets to hang out with cute dogs all day long while working out.

- Babysit your grandbabies, and don't be afraid to or feel guilty about asking for money. You are doing your kids a HUGE service by making sure their kids survive each day and daycare costs a TON—so, even if you charge them, you will still be saving them money.

- Personal assistant, doing house chores or work chores for a few hours a day.

- Need help finding jobs? Check out the website seniorjobbank.org.

Now that you know about the happy place or sweet spot, what comes next? It's time for a DRY RUN or a dress rehearsal of your money. Sound like fun? We do a dry run in two different ways.

1. I am going to challenge you to live on the retirement budget we just put together for a year and see how it feels. We need to make sure this budget is sustainable in the long run. This is a crucial first step, because if this budget isn't realistic, then step #2 is worthless. If this budget is too restrictive, then let's do a dry run of your plan B.

2. Dry run projection. We are going to project what your retirement will look like over the next 20, 30, and even 40 years. Doing this allows you to see why if your retirement expenses aren't true to how you are really going to live, it's a waste. The dry run will be comprised of expenses, income, assets, withdrawal rates, social security, inflation, mortality rates, and investment's returns. During this dry run, we will have to make some assumptions, such as using

the current tax law for income taxes. To go in-depth on this type of planning would fill another book entirely, so I will just say it is so CRITICAL to do this exercise with a financial advisor or professional. I've seen people try to do it on their own with some crazy excel worksheets and it gets MESSY! Just tell me you will see an advisor if you want to do this, so I can calm down! A small mistake in this type of planning can throw your entire retirement on its butt, and you will be left to pick up the pieces.

If you are married, it is key to look at your happy place through the lens of three different scenarios:

1. What if you both live long and happy lives until you are 100?
2. What if one of you passes away at the beginning of retirement?
3. What if the other one passes away at the beginning of retirement?

How do the numbers look in each scenario? The reason we look at the numbers in these three different ways is that the surviving spouse can only keep one of the social securities—the higher one. They might also lose a pension along the way. Let's take a look at Lauren's story, who joined the Retirement Club within one year of retiring.

Lauren worked in the same high school she went to as a teenager. She was a transition coach for special needs children for over 20 years. Needless to say, she was ready for a change of scenery! The problem was despite being an expert in everyone else's transition, she couldn't quite figure out her own! (A fact she quickly pointed out during one of my Retirement Roundtables.) After everyone giggled a bit, she realized she needed help.

We met for a Discovery session to do a thorough assessment of her current financial state in regard to her retirement. At the roundtable, she wrote 12/31/2018 as her retirement date, which was only eight months away. She was ambitious but was ready to do the work needed to make her dreams come true to retire, while also creating a business of her own. She couldn't wait to leave behind the old hallways of her past and embark on an exciting new journey.

Can you relate?

I don't think it was a coincidence either that right after our first section of the club: Properly Funding Your Retirement Lifestyle, she received her pension paperwork. She sent a quick message to me asking...no screaming...for help! There are about eight different pension options for teachers; how the heck was she to decide which to take? Most teachers in her school have taken or will take the highest payout. Sounds good, right? BUT what happens if she dies? Her husband wouldn't receive any more of her income because he would lose a pension and social security, which is about $75,000 a year in income. Her plan would blow up if she passed away within the first 20 years of retirement if she chose the highest payout, aka the single life option. Let's do the math, $75,000 over her life span of 35 years would be a $2.6 million decision or mistake! Don't you think it was worth it for Lauren to reach out for help instead of doing what everyone else did?

I hope you said hell, yes!

Lauren was terrified to make a wrong decision and fail her family. It was a big burden weighing on her, but what comforted her was having someone to go to with these questions and having the support of the club to reassure her. Now she can move past that decision knowing she made it out of confidence, NOT out of fear. She can focus her time on building her retirement business, so she has something to retire to, not just retire from in her career. It's amazing when you retire to a purpose, it makes your transition so much smoother, and you don't feel like you are running from something or that you are failing by retiring.

Let's talk about my good friend and client and fellow club member: Jane. As we discussed, Jane left the corporate world to become a baker, and part of her retirement plan is to make money baking. She loves doing it, but she doesn't quite want to own a bakery. Those hours are scary like we talked about. (And exhausting!) During club sessions, we are finding ways she can make some money doing what she loves without the stressful and very LONG hours.

What about you?

Is there a way you can earn extra money doing what you love to do?

I was recently approached by another financial advisor, who wanted me to buy their book of business. Let's call her Tina. Tina was a very successful advisor but had some personal issues to deal with. She wasn't quite ready to call it quits, but her work had become very mundane and boring. Her business wasn't growing, and it had become stale. Not knowing what to do, she thought selling her business was the next step. She started following me on Facebook, and really enjoyed my messages and videos, which is why she reached out. I see this a lot with business owners especially; they've spent so many years building and building, fostering relationships, that it is hard to walk away. You might also get to a point like Tina when you don't know what the next level is for your business. When retiring seems to be the obvious next step. But does retiring mean you failed? Does it mean you don't care anymore? It doesn't have to; in fact, it might mean it's time to "refine" your business.

You can refine your business, shift it, or create a new entity altogether. After Tina and I met, she was thinking in a whole new way. I breathed new life into new possibilities for her, whether it meant selling her book, reinventing her business, or finding a fresh way to work with people and their money. Tina needed a novel perspective and a resurgence in energy. She needed to find something to retire to even if she stayed in the business in a different capacity. She really didn't want to retire yet; she still had some juice left in her but didn't know which direction to go. Selling just seemed to be the easiest. But is the easiest thing really the best for you? Tina felt like she was running away, calling it quits, and failing at her business. And that was supposed to be the "easy" choice. I didn't want that for her, and I don't want it for you.

Now, Tina has to gain clarity over her next move, and I'm here to help! Even though she is an advisor herself, she couldn't figure it out without outside perspective. In fact, she'll be at my next Retirement Roundtable to help gain clarity on what she really, truly wants for her business. Remember, retirement is its own lifetime; you can try new things or reinvent old things. She still has plenty of time to create a new business, like Lauren, if she wants to.

As you approach your new retirement years, lowering your expenses now can be beneficial in two ways. The first is that it helps you pay off your debts, and bump up your savings, which are both necessary to give you the best chances of retiring without running out of money. The second way is that it helps you learn how to live with lower expenses, so you'll need less money to live on in retirement. These benefits make your retirement planning that much more realistic; instead of guessing how much your expenses will be, now, you will know. As the saying goes: knowledge is power. Knowing puts you in control!

I can't tell you how many big financial and life decisions my husband and I have made with confidence because we know exactly how much we spend each month, what we make, and what the difference is. Buying our house was one of the scariest leaps we took together—we went way over our budget—but after looking at our plan (on numerous occasions!), we knew we could swing it. Since I work with money on a daily basis, I tend to lead us in our decisions. Because of this, sometimes I get nervous I'm going to steer us in a bad direction or take on too much (I tend to be a bit aggressive with our investments!). I've learned to include him in more of the decisions and discuss pros and cons openly with him. Having the proof of our income and expenses each month always helps us make decisions out of security and not out of fear and emotions.

In the end, you do NOT get what you truly want when you make life and money decisions out of fear. Those decisions tend to be rash and quick when you feel trapped by fear, stress, and anxiety. I call it tunnel vision when you forget all the options you really do have in your current situation. When you go through your expenses and income, you might feel tight or restricted, but remember, you always have a choice. Take a step back and identify your choices, which will help you feel financial freedom. The opposite of freedom is feeling trapped, which means you have no choices available. Let me remind you that you always have choices; you just need help identifying them.

I love crunching the numbers, and then crunching them again and again until we find a way to make your decisions work for you. In other words, how can we raise your income, lower your expenses, and make your retirement dreams a reality? It's helpful to have your income buckets ready, meaning, what your expenses will be, and what your plan B is in case your plan A isn't a possibility at the moment. Remember as you get closer to retirement, you start trading money for time. Having clarity over what is more important to you and what is realistic will always bring your focus back to what matters.

My FREE retirement workbook will help you realize the possibilities in your life.

You can access it at www.strongretirementclub.com/free-workbook to get started crunching your own numbers!

Knowing the ins and outs of your numbers helps prevent the biggest risk to your retirement...REGRET—which is what our next chapter is all about!

Chapter 5: Don't Regret the Chances You Don't Take

◊◊◊

"And one day she discovered that she was fierce and strong. And full of fire. And that not even she could hold herself back."
~Mark Anthony

Let's cut right to the heart of the matter and talk about the BIGGEST risk in your life, and especially in your retirement.

REGRET!

I hosted a Retirement Roundtable and asked the women what is the biggest risk in retirement? "Regret" was the initial comment. Regret of retiring too soon or too late. Regret of not spending money, regret of spending too much. Regret of not spending enough time with your loved ones, regret of spending too much time with them. Regret that you waited too long to tackle your bucket list items or did them all too quickly.

What do all these things have in common? Your health!

Think about it.

If you retire too soon, you might think your health will fail you in your later years, and so you retire to do activities like travel. If you retire too late, your health might be too poor to do what's on your bucket list. Your health allows you to do more or less of what you love to do.

If you spend too little of your money that might be because you thought you'd live longer. If you spend too much, it might be because you lived longer than you thought. Your health was too good or not good enough.

If you spent too much time with your loved ones, it's because you thought they or you wouldn't live as long. If you didn't spend enough time, it's because your health failed you quicker than you anticipated.

"Your wealth is your health." What a perfect quote to sum it all up! All of your savings, all of your bucket list items are worthless if you don't have your health.

Let me ask you this...are you afraid of:

Being too tired to do things in retirement?

Feeling unmotivated?

Not being able to drive?

Losing your independence?

Falling or having an injury?

Feeling isolated and alone, with no social interaction?

Not being able to go on the trips or enjoy the money you worked so hard for?

Having your family worry about you ALL THE TIME?

If so, let's get serious about your health. The KEY to a happy retirement is maintaining your health and making your quality of life a priority! As you approach retirement, your priorities will shift. Money seems less important, and that big paycheck even seems less valuable, yet your health will become center stage!

I recently met with a couple who were close to retirement, especially the husband, Bob. Bob could tell his mental capacity was diminishing, and he wanted to retire within a year. It was just that he couldn't keep up anymore, but he also wanted to enjoy his retirement and his health while he still had it! On the flip side, his wife, Sally, wanted to work longer. I explained to both of them since they were on such separate pages with their retirement goals and timeline, that while his quality of life will improve once he retires, her quality of life might diminish if she leaves too soon.

They had never thought of their situation like that before. She wants to keep working because it will keep her engaged and social and continue to challenge her mentally. But working will only make Bob's health worse, and he needs more free time to improve his well-being. As you can tell, there isn't one solution for everyone when it comes to retirement, even for a couple!

Do you think you will regret that you will retire too soon? One woman at my Retirement Roundtable was thinking about retiring within a year or so but just isn't sure. She fears she will regret leaving and being bored at home or missing her job. This tells me that she isn't ready to leave work completely, but maybe it's time to refine her current job. I've seen this a lot in situations where women are DONE with their current work schedule, responsibilities, and so on, and want to do something else. If this rings a bell, you are ready to REFINE your life to something simpler, more fulfilling, and fun!

Another woman regretted that she waited too long to leave the workforce. I know this regret far too well because of what happened to a family member. He was thinking of retiring for a while, and I kept asking, "Why wait?" He had dealt with health issues his entire life, and I wanted him to enjoy his retirement as long as he could. When he finally decided to retire, he was so excited! Then he found himself in the hospital a few months before retirement. He was in and out of the hospital for a while until one morning, when we got the call that he didn't wake up. His funeral was the day of his retirement party at work.

So, you can see why I am so passionate about this risk and preventing it as much as possible. We kept saying, "If he'd only had one year to fully enjoy his life, and go hiking, fishing, and biking because he just LOVED the outdoors." Please take your health into consideration when you think about when to retire. I don't want this same ending for you.

Regret can be a very uneasy, you either go for what you want, or you regret not going for it. Are there things in your life you regret doing or not doing? What pushed you to make the decision whether to go through with a choice or not? A lot of times, we regret the risks we didn't take. Retirement can be a risk, I'm not going to lie, BUT the bigger risk might be trading your healthy days on this Earth for money. To help you decide whether to retire now or later, you need to start understanding: What are you prioritizing NOW? What is more important to you? Do you want to earn more money or earn your time back in retirement?

Take a moment to write down your top 5 priorities in your life:

1. _____

2. _____

3. _____

4. _____

5. _____

Where does money fall on your list? Where does health fall on your list? Where does family fall?

Next, write down what you want to start prioritizing:

1. _____

2. _____

3. _____

4. _____

5. _____

Once you've decided your course of action, it's time to go for it! We'll begin with how to stay active, engaged, and social in retirement during each stage, as well as what to focus on in your health in each stage.

Honeymoon Stage

During the Honeymoon Stage in retirement, you will have the inner conflict of whether you should retire now or later. What will you prioritize, money, or health? Money or time? Unless you retire with health benefits, your healthcare costs will likely be costly! Is it worth it to you to spend out of pocket for coverage, or would you rather work somewhere just to be covered? Some women in my club are willing to work, but at a less stressful job, to have the employee benefits or at least to cover the costs of their coverage. If you've never paid for your own health insurance, then you might not realize how much money it will be. You can expect to pay anywhere from $7,000 to $10,000-plus a year in health insurance premiums in addition to out-of-pocket costs.

I'll let that sink in for you!

Your expenses will come down to your health, what type of doctors you go to, what type of drugs you take, and your income.

Most women are terrified to leave their high paycheck because it is hard to walk away from that money. They figure they will work until 65 or as close as they can get to it without losing their sanity to make it to Medicare age! BUT what they don't think about is this: what if you leave and get a lower paying job, but you love it? You love it enough to continue working past age 65, and that means you'll work longer. If you work longer, it means you will pull less money out of your retirement funds. Taking this road can be a breakeven for these women!

During the Honeymoon Stage, you may need to get your own healthcare coverage until you reach age 65. Once you reach 65, you will have a 7-month enrollment window to grab your Medicare coverage without getting penalized. If you miss your window, it will cost you! Your premiums will increase for life! As you can tell, it is so important to be well-educated during retirement to avoid mistakes such as these. Now that you are retired remember you have time as a luxury! You can focus your energy on putting your health first, getting fit and active, and prioritizing enough time to make healthy meals! I've heard from several concerned family members of recently retired women who keep having health issues. They aren't even able to enjoy the BEST time of their life because their health keeps getting in the way. I know you don't want this, which is why I team up with health and fitness coaches who focus their efforts on women near and in retirement. If you need a contact to get started, let me know! There are a few experts in my Facebook Group that you can access here: **The Retirement Suite** (http://bit.ly/TheRetirementSuiteGroup) and who are ready to help out! I love bringing them into my club to talk with the members about making their health a priority.

Relaxation Stage

The Relaxation Stage follows the Honeymoon Stage, and when you arrive here, you will want to slow down a bit. You might slow down because your health won't let you keep up or because you want to maintain your health! Just when you think you should slow down with your fitness routine retirement might be the time to up it! But before you do anything different, always listen to your body and doctor! You'll notice when you are so busy, you become stressed, and stress is never good for your health, especially when it's excessive and never-ending! You might even need to schedule some NOTHING time on your calendar to take care of yourself and rest up. What I've found during this time of retirement is that women have unexpected health issues. You might need a knee or hip replacement; you might have a stroke, heart attack, or arthritis. When you go through health scares, you are forced to leave your retirement routine to recover. You must be careful if this happens! When you leave a routine, you'll feel alone and isolated, which can lead to depression. Depression then contributes to more health issues and declining mental health. Remember to always maintain some social connection and engagement when you are recovering.

As a side note to the Relaxation Stage, we've noticed one of the bigger retirement expenses takes place during this time. There seems to be a HUGE trend in dental costs. New teeth are expensive and are almost never included in a retirement plan. You've been warned! But seriously, be careful when you are at the dentist, and make sure you fully understand the costs associated with your new set of teeth. People always argue their spending will decrease once they are out of the Honeymoon stage because they won't travel as much. We don't see this at all; your spending will change, yes. But you will still be spending the same or similar amounts!

Reflection Stage

Lastly, the Reflection Stage will be the time when your health starts to decline. You may need a home health aide, assisted living facility, or nursing home. OR your partner will need help. There are so many logistics that accompany this stage from funding the extra help to making sure your belongings don't get lost in the shuffle! How will you find the right nursing home facility, pay for it, and ensure your bills and belongings won't get forgotten? And how do you make sure it all happens without burdening your children? Further, what if you don't have children to help with those decisions? These are all great questions which will get answered in this section.

BUT remember, the Reflection Stage doesn't have to be so daunting. If it is done right, you can still be partying it up in the nursing home! At my last Retirement Roundtable, the ladies all agreed that this is the time to grab a NEW boyfriend and shake things up! Don't worry; I won't tell anyone...

Before we got into the nitty-gritty of our Retirement Health Plans during our session, we went over our general health! Without your health, your money and your bucket list, won't be put into action! It is CRITICAL to implement healthy habits as you transition into retirement to help ensure your health won't fail you but only improve. And yes, your health can improve with age, trust me! Let's get you started on this next exercise by identifying three health goals for the New Year. It can be to drink more water, join a gym, or add strength training to your health plan.

Health Goals:

1._____

2._____

3._____

Next, how will you get stretchy?

How will you stretch yourself beyond what you are comfortable doing to reach your goals.

Here is an example: Maybe you are nervous about joining a new gym. It can be so intimidating, so you get insecure, and think everyone will judge your clothes or your lifting technique, and that you will feel stupid, right? I've been there many times! Your stretchy moment will be to join a gym and strut your butt into the place to put your health goals into action.

How about finding a therapist to talk to about your weight issues? This can be *very* stretchy for some people. It is quite uncomfortable to open up about the health issues you've had in the past to a stranger and hope they get your concerns. But without opening up to this stranger, you may never overcome your weight insecurities. So, I challenge you to get stretchy and reach beyond your comfort zone. Everything you want in life is outside of your comfort zone, after all; otherwise, we would all have everything we want! But to get what we want in life; we have to stretch ourselves! So, Stretch! I promise; it isn't as scary as you think!

Three ways you will stretch yourself:

1._____

2._____

3._____

To understand where you are going with your goals and what you want to accomplish with them, you have to think about your overall health vision. Picture yourself 10 years into retirement. How do you want to look and feel? Do you want even more energy than you have now, less stress, and less cushion in your butt? Dream about the NEW and retired you...who does that look like? Understanding your vision will help you make a lot of key decisions about your health. When you have a difficult question to solve, such as *should I eat donuts every morning or a protein shake*, go back to your vision. I do this with my work. For years, I had no clue of my vision. I ended up taking on too many opportunities and driving myself (and my husband) nuts from being pulled in too many directions. Now that I know my overall vision is a Full-Service Retirement Suite with different professionals to help my clients on an entirely new and never before seen level, I can make better decisions going forward.

When I need a little more insight into what choice I should make, I always ask myself: *will this choice take me closer or farther from my vision?*

Vision:

_____

_____

_____

_____

Lastly, it always comes back to our WHY. Why is it so important to hit these goals, get stretchy, and develop your vision? Why do you want to stay healthy? It might be to tackle your long bucket list of travels. Or to enjoy your grandchildren and great-grandchildren. My why is because I want to make a bigger impact on the women I work with. I want to transform all of their lives, open them up to new possibilities, and give them the best retirement ever. My why also concerns my daughter and being a role model (or role mommy) to look up to. I want to not just have a successful career, but a *significant* career, one that really matters to everyone it touches upon. What is your why?

Why:

_____

_____

_____

_____

As you enter the next section of this book, we will dissect your health plan and build it out in a simple and easy to follow method using my Retirement Stages!

What really helped the women in the Strong Retirement Club™ (https://www.strongretirementclub.com/) was to build out their Health Plan. Their Health Plan not only covered the traditional healthcare costs associated with pre and post-Medicare, but also included the costs of staying fit and healthy!

During our Health and Long-Term Care As You Age Topic, we built our plan for each of the three stages of retirement. We noted it helped to piece down your plans into sizeable chunks, so you knew exactly what to cover and when. Instead of throwing everything together into an overwhelming plan, we could put each puzzle piece into a timeline of when each person needed to think about the issue, how much it would cost them, and when to implement it. How does that sound?

Here is an example of one member's plan:

Honeymoon:

- **Health Components**
  - **Pre Medicare:** length of time before Medicare: 3 years until 65
    - Price per month $800 per year $10,800
  - **Medicare:** Enrollment Window: 7-month window, birthday is in April, so enrollment window is from January until July.
    - Price of Medicare per year: $1,461.60 (based on income)
    - Price of supplement: $4,800 per year
- **Nutrition and Fitness**
  - Social: Participate in gym fitness classes, join women's club
  - Physical: Join gym, add strength training.
  - Mental: Volunteer using skills from my career, join book club, start journaling.
  - Food Plan: Change sugar and carb intake, more balanced meals throughout the day, more water to diet!
  - Rest and Recovery: Add meditation to morning rituals.
- **Long Term Care**
  - Action Steps: Start family discussion around my thoughts and goals for needing Long-Term Care later in retirement. Meet with estate attorney to further discuss options.
- **Unexpected Conditions and Costs**
  - Surgeries: Need hip surgery within next year.
  - Dental: Need new caps, estimated cost about $7,000.

- Physical Therapy: Will need for 12 weeks after surgery. Look into how much own health insurance will cover.

Relaxation:

- **Health Components**
  - **Medicare:** Renewal Window: General Enrollment Window January 1st until March 31st
    - Price of Medicare per year: $1,461.60 (based on income)
    - Price of supplement: $4,800 per year
- **Nutrition and Fitness**
  - Social: Participate in gym fitness classes, active member in women's club.
  - Physical: Continue at the gym, add stability work.
  - Mental: Leader of book club, write my own book!
  - Food Plan: Iron-rich foods, more fiber, and continue with water (and wine!) intake.
  - Rest and Recovery: Continue with meditation in the morning.
- **Long Term Care**
  - Action Steps: Have another family discussion about what will be happening in the next few years. All estate documents: will, power of attorney, and living will to be updated. Create Irrevocable Living Trust and move house and certain non-retirement assets into trust. This will start the 5-year look back clock to qualify for Medicare. Explain this to family members and the trust's trustee!
- **Unexpected Conditions and Costs**
  - Surgeries: Hopefully none!
  - Dental: Hopefully none! But realistically, more caps with an estimated cost of $10,000.

- Physical Therapy: To be determined!

Reflection:

- **Health Components**
    - **Medicare:** Renewal Window: General Enrollment Window January 1st until March 31st
        - Price of Medicare per year: $1,461.60 (based on income)
        - Price of supplement: $4,800 per year
    - **Nutrition and Fitness**
        - Social: Participate in group games, not Bingo—I hate Bingo! Visit with family and friends for extended stays.
        - Physical: Daily walks, strength training, and stability work.
        - Mental: Work on my second book!
        - Food Plan: Continue with wine (I mean water), intake!
        - Rest and Recovery: Continue with meditation in the morning.
    - **Long-Term Care**
        - Action Steps: Additional family discussion to address any needs at the moment; I would like to stay at home for at least two years with a home health aide. Finish transferring assets into my Living Irrevocable Trust. Find nursing home and discuss the payment plan to reserve my spot and buy into it. What will be the initial down deposit? What will the cost be every month? Will the monthly rate increase?
        - Logistics
            - Housing: Sell the house right before entering the nursing home.
            - Costs: Retirement assets will cover initial monthly payments for the nursing home. The equity from my

house will pay for the down deposit into the nursing home.

- Extra Help: Use organizer on file, enroll Bill Pay help specialist, and Medicaid specialist to help qualify for Medicaid.
- Belongings: Nieces and nephews will receive all photo albums and videos.
  - What to sell: all furniture besides Mom's cabinet.
  - What to keep: Mom's china and her cabinet!
  - What to donate: Old kitchen table and family room furniture.
- **Unexpected Conditions and Costs**
  - Surgeries: To be announced!
  - Dental: Don't care anymore!
  - Physical Therapy: Probably!

Remember! "Having a plan in place leaves you less vulnerable!"

Resources!

- Pre Medicare Health Insurance: https://www.healthcare.gov/
- Medicare Enrollment Periods: https://medicare.com/enrollment/medicare-enrollment-periods/
- Medigap Plans: https://www.mymedigapplans.com/medicare-supplement-plans/new-jersey/

Chapter 6: Hoping to be Secure is Not Security

◊◊◊

"I don't believe in luck. It's persistence, hard work, and not forgetting your dream."
~Janet Jackson

How does your refinement all come together? Just like we give your life purpose in retirement, we also give your money purpose. It's time to look at all the retirement components you will have to deal with, and check how many of these variables, your money will cover. When you think about your health, the variables in your refinement it affects include Long Term Care costs, inflation, and living too long. Your lifestyle can put your money at risk, your legacy at risk, and your family at risk. Everything gets intertwined with the different variables in your retirement. How do they all work, how do they affect one another, and how do you make your money work FOR you? Which brings you to our final piece...putting it all together!

Don't get overwhelmed!

Do you ever get so overwhelmed with all the decisions you have to make in retirement? I know this happens a lot with retirement planning, and I'm here to help!

Where to live?
What to do with your money?
What the heck to do with your social security?

So many questions to answer and decisions to make. How do you know what are the best choices for you and your retirement?

I felt the same way when I was pregnant with so many details to figure out. You have thoughts on how to parent, what room should be the nursery, what name to give your kid, and what type of nipple to use for the bottles! But then our daughter came, and we realized the most important aspect of our plan was our willingness to adjust it. Some days it felt like we were adjusting it every minute, while other times, we would get a few days at a stretch before our next tweak!

Are you open to changing your current retirement course?

If you are committed to living your best life in retirement, then this is the number one prequalification! A willingness for change, to hear a new perspective, and to do it with ease will take you toward the finish line.

Sound good?

I love my Strong Retirement Club™ for so many reasons; I love the community we have created, the connections the women are making with each other and the other professionals in it. I'm a huge fan of educating women, building their confidence, and giving them back control over their lives.

Our motto is Community, Confidence, and Control because we aim to give you that in return for joining the club. Our business's value is building a community of trust, safety, and vulnerability because we know only then will there be real change in your life! The Strong Retirement Club™ is about giving women a different level of support, education, and community from the traditional financial planning role we too often see.

My second love of the club is how much it is pushing me to be a better retirement advisor and help not only the women in my club but also the women I help one on one. I've learned one of the BIGGEST benefits for me has been the knowledge I've learned and applied to the club. I can now use that knowledge with my individual clients to better serve them. The information and experience I've gained from building the Club helps all the women in the club AND all my one on one clients to execute their retirement goals and dreams so much more efficiently and effectively! All the women who benefit from my new strategies, tips, and applications, finally feel like it all makes sense. They no longer are forcing the separate puzzle pieces either. And they aren't forcing planning with their money or stuck worrying about what is out of their control. We focus on the components of your life and retirement that you can control, and we work on those instead of stressing over markets, inflation, taxes, and long-term care costs.

Can you think of a time when you felt like you were forcing a situation? A relationship that should have ended? A house that didn't make sense for your family? A job you wanted to make work, but didn't in the end? The same can be said for you and your money. Do you ever feel like you are forcing things? If you are shaking your head, then your money is NOT being very effective or efficient. Your money should always be working FOR you, NOT against you. I want your money working for you, and if you are open to learning, let's find a more effective and more efficient way to manage your hard-earned money!

When you think about retirement, what are all the components you have to manage?

The short list:

Lifestyle
Health
Legacy planning
Money

Now, let's examine your lifestyle needs:

Social life
Travel
Where you will live
How much you will work
Etc.

Health:

Healthcare costs
How to stay healthy and active
Mental health
Long-term care
Etc.

Estate:

Documents you need
How you want to leave your loved ones
All the tough questions about how you want to leave this world

Once we start digging in, you can appreciate how deep down the retirement rabbit hole you can go.

When it comes to your money, what are all the variables that will make up your retirement plan?

- Income: how much income will you receive, from where, and for how long?
- Expenses: how much will your lifestyle cost you for the length of your retirement?
- Taxes: yes, retirees still pay a good amount of taxes!
- Inflation: how will inflation reduce the purchasing power of your money? Healthcare inflation is higher than traditional inflation on average.
- Assets: how much have you saved up so far for retirement funding?

- Withdrawal Rates: based on the size of your assets and the income you need to cover your expenses, what is your withdrawal rate? Divide the income you need from your assets by the size of your assets = your withdrawal rate percentage. If you withdraw 4% from your investments to live on in retirement, and you have $1,000,000 saved up, you will withdraw $40,000 from your account. This is your withdrawal rate!
- Investment Returns: what type of return is your money earning on an annual basis?
- Required Minimum Distributions: at age 70 ½, the IRS forces you to take money out of your retirement plans (not Roth IRAs).

Now that you have an outline of the variables, what exactly does it all mean? How do they work together? Let's look at the variables that are working FOR you!

Your income is your greatest money variable working for you.

It can come in different forms such as pension income, social security, rental income, part-time work, and even your investments. It allows you to withdraw less from your investment account, which helps with the risk of living long into your retirement; it helps to fund long-term care costs later in retirement; it can leave a bigger legacy for your family. The less money you have to withdraw to live on, the better your chances are to not run out of money later in your retirement. The better the chances you will have more money to help fund your Long-Term Care Costs. The better the chances you will have money to pass onto your loved ones. And the biggest reason you need to know the intricacies of your income sources is...to have fun with them! Some retirees work just to fund their travels, go out to eat, or gift it to their family. Income can become extra money or splurge money if you plan your finances right!

Most women I work with like to "transition" into retirement. Meaning, they do some type of work after leaving their busy and hectic careers. They might take up substitute teaching like one woman in our retirement club, who just couldn't deal with the politics at work or the extra projects she brought home every night and on weekends. Karen still loved the children and teaching, so we found a way for her to continue teaching children but without the hassle of pleasing the higher-ups! Yes, if you go this route, you'll have to accept lower pay, but if you can find a way to work on your terms for less pay, would that be worth it to you? A lot of women say yes! They love the idea of having some type of job to bring money in, but with less stress and fewer hours.

Good or even great investment returns can do wonders for your overall plan.

Let's imagine the stock market has a stellar year, and your investments go up more than normal! That's exciting news, BUT how do we best use this extra money? Do you want to put it toward your next big dental bill? Heck no! Let's enhance our strategy by giving the extra money more than one purpose!

One club member, Lisa, likes to use the extra money to cushion her risk of living too long. She'll put the extra gains back into her investments, so she'll hopefully have more money working for her, and her scariest risk of longevity is something that tends to happen to her family. They all seem to live well into their 90s! This is important to her because she doesn't have children and has always been independent. Her fear is becoming dependent on someone, and she has no idea who that someone would be. I've learned when you live independently for so long; the most frightening event is if you become dependent because it is an unknown. When you don't know what it's like to be dependent, you can feel like a burden, and it can scare the heck out of you! So, if you are like Lisa, make sure you prioritize longevity risk when you put your investment plan together!

The lower your expenses are, the more money you will have working for you. This means more of your income can be used for fun; you will withdraw less from your investments, leaving more in place to grow for you. The biggest benefit of low expenses is this...less stress! Less stress on you as a person, less stress on your money, and a whole lot less stress when the markets have a bad year. One woman in our club, we will call her Lauren, made it a point to pay off her mortgage before retirement. It has freed her up to save more for retirement while spending more on trips before retirement, BUT the biggest pay off has been the reduction of stress. She is single, and her expenses are solely her responsibility, so if something happens to her job, then it is on her to make sure her debts are paid. Knowing her biggest expense has been paid off would take the stress of losing a job or changing jobs away. Do you agree? It has made Lauren's money more efficient, reduced stress, and given her more play money. I call that a win on three fronts!

If income is working for us, what is working AGAINST you?

Inflation

Unfortunately, in retirement, there are more items working against you than for you. Inflation is typically 3%, and health care inflation is 5%, you may not see the value of your dollars impacted by this at the beginning of your retirement but give it a few years and you will! Inflation slowly eats away at your dollars, especially if you keep a good amount of money (more than 20% of your assets), in the bank or under your mattress (please don't keep any money under your mattress!). Most of your income is on a fixed schedule, so inflation can take its toll on your money given enough time. Investments are a way to mitigate this risk, but you also need to make sure you aren't betting it all on the market because doing this leads to the market volatility risk discussed below!

Women tend to be conservative with their money and investments, which translates into TOO much money sitting in your bank account. If you are shaking your head at this, then listen up because you aren't going to like what I have to say. As I told Lisa and another new club member, "Money sitting in your bank account is working against you in two BIG ways. The first is you still have to pay taxes on the little amount you actually do earn. Second, inflation erodes away your money in the bank each year."

If we break this down, it can look like this: If your bank account earns you 1%, yet inflation is 3%, and healthcare inflation is 5%, then what are you left with? Negative 2% and 4%! You should always have a cushion in your bank account equaling six months to one year of living expenses in retirement, BUT make sure your money is working FOR you as well as with your other investments!

We advised these two club members, to leave their cushion in their savings account while investing other in a more tax efficient way to help protect against longevity, pay for Long-Term Care costs, and protect against market volatility!

Let's count how many purposes we gave that money sitting in the bank account: Tax Efficient =1, Longevity=1, Long Term Care=1, and Market Volatility =1 for a total of 4 purposes! Instead of 2 variables working against you, NOW we have 4 working FOR you! That is why I call it multi-tasking your money to ease your life!

Are you curious now how we can do this for your own money?

Taxes!

I'm sorry to say this, but in retirement, you will still pay taxes. You will owe money on any withdrawals from traditional 401(k) plans and IRAs. If you work, you will owe taxes; if you receive a pension, you will owe taxes; even some of your social security benefit can be taxed. How you manage your taxes and tax rate is in your control and your responsibility. Smart withdrawal strategies, income planning, and tax work can make your money more effective and tax-efficient!

In retirement, you get to retire with a partner and that partner is...Uncle Sam. He likes to share in your savings and income in retirement. Are taxes a concern of yours? I know it was for a few club members, which is why we brought in an accountant to help keep people from overpaying in their taxes. When you are tax conscious, it leaves more money for fun, but also for your legacy, to counter longevity risk, and so much more. Or maybe you just want to keep as much of your hard-earned money as you can? I don't blame you!

Taxes come into play again when your Required Minimum Distribution begins when you turn the lucky age of 70 ½! Be proactive and implement some strategies such as Roth IRA Conversions to help lower your tax liability later in retirement when these withdrawals begin. The same club member we spoke about before, Lauren, makes a small conversion from her IRA into her Roth IRA every year to help lower the amount she will be forced to take out of her IRA when her RMD is due.

Market Volatility

Market volatility is a normal occurrence in the markets; they go up, and they go down. You can manage it, but that is up to you to employ the right financial advisor and investment structure for your money. Having the right strategy in place is critical to reducing the volatility in your money, especially for the money you are using to pay your retirement expenses.

Are you nervous that the year you retire, the stock market will plummet? Market volatility can take a huge chunk out of your investments, especially when you are withdrawing money to live on. Suzie, a client, was nervous that the year she retired would be the last good year in the markets. This fear of doomsday in the markets kept her from retiring. We put together a model for her money with different buckets for each year of retirement. Her first few years were very conservative, so even if the markets went straight down for three or even five years, her monthly income wouldn't be impacted. Would this strategy make you feel more secure leading up to retirement like it did for Suzie?

Expenses

High expenses and withdrawal rates go hand in hand. The more your lifestyle costs you, the more you need to withdraw from your accounts. We have seen that this is the number one reason people are running out of money in retirement. Retirees aren't planning properly and are spending more than they ever planned for. It is a huge risk and something we talk about extensively in our club, merging your lifestyle with your money to make sure they are aligned while not adding to your retirement risks.

Luckily for you, expenses can always be adjusted as long as you remember the KEY piece: being open to adjusting your plan! Where you spend money is always a choice. As Karen, a club member, approached her retirement, we met to see if she could swing her current expenses based on what her retirement income would be. Seeing how her current, monthly expenses would eat into her travel money each month, she decided it wasn't worth it to stay in her house. She made a choice to spend less on daily expenses so she can have more to travel with.

Longevity

Longevity is a variable we cannot control, although we can try to manage it a bit with good health and good money management. The longer you live, the more money it will cost you, which is why finding the right products and income strategy is a crucial factor in helping to protect you against this risk.

Do you have longevity in your family? My grandmother lived to 98 while her sister lived to 100, so longevity is on my mind! Do you want to risk it and live for today or properly plan out your retirement in case you live beyond 85? Most women in my world want to be conservative with their planning because the last thing we want is to be a burden on our kids at age 90! And what if they don't have kids? Then they really want to have a well thought out plan in place! So, we look at what alternative investments can help protect outliving your money.

Long Term Care

Long-Term Care is a huge risk to any retirement plan because it is so expensive, and we can control only so much of it. The good news is there are many ways to help plan for the risk of needing Long-Term Care for you and partner, and even if your parents may need it. Talk with an advisor and an estate or elder care attorney to make sure you are properly prepared for this big risk that can work against you and your money. You can find ways to protect against it or manage it.

Have you ever dealt with a parent in a nursing home? Usually, women are very concerned about long-term care because they've witnessed how expensive their parent's extra care is. There is a 58% chance of women needing a nursing home.[1] I'd like you to take out a coin; heads mean you go into a nursing home and tails means you won't need a nursing home. Flip the coin and see what your outcome is. This is how quickly your life can turn, just as fast as that coin. That means you have very little time to plan out what you will need if you should need extra care. The time to plan is now! This is the time to think about these questions: How will you pay for the extra care? What type of care will you want or need? Where do you want the care to take place?

When we have an idea as to the answers to these questions, we can then back into how much money we will need available to plan for your Long-Term Care Costs.

With all of these variables or risks working against you, you can either protect against them, manage them, or neutralize them. The first step is to read through them and mark which ones give you the most stress or worry. We want to prioritize what is important in your retirement plan.

Take a moment to think through these questions:

What will make you feel secure in retirement?
What has to happen to make you feel secure?
And who can help?

My approach is to look at your money and assess how many of these risks can we manage, protect, or neutralize with one investment strategy. It's a big job, but I love it!

I love seeing how many purposes we can give your money to help it work with you and not against you. It's exciting that we can give your money more than one purpose to make it more effective and efficient—which is the name of the game in retirement. If you don't know how many of these variables your money is covering, then you need a second opinion! I'd like to invite you to have a call with me to gain clarity on which variables make you most nervous, and how your money can help you feel secure and stable as you approach retirement. Sound good?

Book your call at www.jessicaweaver.setmore.com.

Your homework is to take out your retirement journal and reflect on these questions!

1. How will I feel secure in my retirement?

_____

_____

_____

_____

_____

2. What needs to happen to feel secure?

_____

_____

_____

_____

_____

3. Who can help me implement these steps?

_____

_____

_____

_____

Chapter 7: Bring the Future into the Present

◊◊◊

"I alone cannot change the world, but I can cast a stone across the water to create many ripples."
~ Mother Teresa

How does one even begin the process of estate planning? What goes into estate planning, and do I really need to think about my death?

I once heard a financial advisor say their favorite aspect of the job is estate planning. Curious why death was their favorite part, I asked her to explain the reasoning behind it. She simply said: "It is usually the first time in the conversation when it goes from being about the client and shifts to being about their family." Thank you, Tiffany, for that perspective!

Estate planning, or as I like to call it Legacy Planning, isn't about you or me. It is about those around you, and once you can switch your mindset to this belief, you won't go into this element of retirement thinking about your demise! That's because it is no longer about you...it is about all those *around you*. In our Club, we talk about leaving a bigger impact on the world when you are no longer here.

Question: How do you make more ripples after your death than when you were alive?

Answer: By properly leaving a legacy to the world when you pass away. Again, once you decide to live by your legacy; you will no longer be scared of what is next after your life. You might still be sad, and feel as if you will miss out, but you will KNOW those around you will be taken care of in a way you might not have ever been able to do while you were with them.

By now, we've gone through the three stages of Retirement: the Honeymoon, the Relaxation, and the Reflection. During the Reflection Stage, you begin a journey of looking back on your life and thinking about what type of life you have lived. No matter how many or how few regrets you have, you always have a choice to make a lasting impact on this world. Do you want to wait until the reflection stage to do this, or do you want to start now?

Let's start now! I know personally, I cannot even fathom not being around to see my daughter grow old, get married, and have babies. I am just so excited to see what type of woman she grows up to be. I also know I NEVER want to think about not being with my hubby, Eric, and I definitely don't want to think of him remarrying if I pass away early. BUT what I do know is this: I have done so much in my legacy planning that not only will my daughter and husband be even better off if I pass away (thanks to lots of life insurance!), but they will also have so many memories, handwritten letters, cards, pictures, as well as tokens and mementos that they will never be able to forget me. *You heard me, Eric, I will haunt you until the end!* Just kidding.

There are so many ways that we can leave legacies every day.

Let me share what I mean by talking about examples in my own life.

To begin, there is all of my writings, my books, my blog postings, and my videos. My hope is someone special will take all of it, and continue building onto our #pinkfix movement (if you haven't gotten involved yet, go to our Facebook and Instagram to check it out!), as well as my Strong Retirement Club™, Not Your Father's blog, and all the training that helps numerous women long after I am gone! Because it isn't about you and me, it is about all the women impacted, helped, and supported by it.

We Are Family

My family's favorite way to spend time is by taking trips together! We remember all of our vacations by getting Christmas ornaments. Then every year when we decorate the tree, (something I always make sure we do together!), we look back on those amazing memories. With every wine bottle I open, I write on the cork a goal or affirmation. Then on New Year's Eve, we go through them to see which ones came true, and we put the ones still to come back in the glass container. We start the year with some goals to fulfill, and then we add more with each bottle. We also bought a case of wine for the year we were married and will do the same for the year our daughter was born. On big anniversaries, special birthdays, and celebrations, we will open a bottle. Can you guess what we will do with our corks?

My favorite Christmas was Andie's first Christmas with us. It was the year my first book came out, and I decided to get a few hardcover books created. I wrote a special note in each book for my parents, in-laws, Eric, and Andie. It was a way to thank them for their support during one of the best yet craziest years of our lives! But it also showed them how much my work integrates with my family. I wouldn't be doing what I love if it wasn't for my family, and their love and support. But I also wanted them to know they support me in being my best self when I am around them. Loving my job has allowed me to live my best life at work AND at home.

You see, estate planning goes beyond the typical will and life insurance! It's about your relationships, and ties with your community and your work. How can you leave a bigger impact on this world, validate the relationships that are important to you, and leave knowing everyone around you is taken care of?

Estate planning begins with your priorities. I just met with a woman who will retire in a year. She asked me whether people in retirement use life insurance. Simple question, yet hard to answer! It gets complex because everyone is different! A couple's need for life insurance is different from that of a single person. A person with children is different from that of a person without children. Someone with limited assets might want life insurance in case they spend all their money in retirement and want to make sure their children or grandchildren will still inherit. My answer was life insurance can be used in retirement, but we need to figure out what the purpose of it is, which brings us back to priorities!

Do you know what your estate planning priorities are? What is the most important thing you want or NEED to happen when you pass away?

To help you answer these questions and more surrounding estate planning, I sat down with my friend, Mary Beth.

Meet Mary Beth

Mary Beth is a Financial Planner with a passion for Legacy Planning, as well as she is a #1 Best Selling Author of the book: *Leaving a Legacy of Love*. Her expertise is incredible, and she brings a refreshing perspective on estate planning, which is why she is included in this book. Mary Beth is one of my closest friends, and I have so much respect and admiration for the woman she is. Life hasn't been easy for her, yet she is the most grateful, caring, and open-hearted person I know. Thank you for being a part of my life, and our book!

Jess: Mary Beth, when did you get started with making legacy planning your focus?

Mary Beth: I always was interested. When I came on as an advisor 12 years ago, it fascinated me, but I really only put it into focus in the last couple of years because I realized how many people were actually lacking a plan of some sort. I saw the negative effects on people, my clients, people that I care about.

Jess: You saw the repercussions of people who didn't have any estate document or a will or maybe a poorly drafted will?

Mary Beth: Yes. That was the sad part, but I also saw, on the flip side, the ease and appreciation of someone actually planning well for the family. Doing this just made the process easier for the people left behind because they were grieving, and they had to take on this new role. Since there was a plan in place, they could lean on the attorney, the CPA, and the financial advisor for advice and guidance, which made the transition a little bit easier for them.

Jess: What I've noticed is when you plan it out properly and really make it a point in your financial plan or any type of life plan and you have your will done, a power of attorney, all the components—and we'll get into that—it allows you to properly grieve and be in the moment versus worrying about what's happening with the money. Or worrying about how are bills going to get paid; how is the money going to get divided, and are you and your siblings going to fight over things? Is that what you've seen, that people can genuinely be there with their family during such a tough time?

Mary Beth: That is a big component. I would have to say that the biggest relief I see in people is when I can say to them, "Listen, these are the three things you have to do now, but then the rest can wait. Just be with your family, relax. There's not a rush. It takes time, anyway." When there is a plan in place, it's more comforting for the family because there are a few things you have to do up front, immediately, as you know, but there are others that can wait. When you make a plan, there's not a mad rush, and it makes life easier for the person who's going to be in charge.

Jess: It's important for people to remember that they really don't have to rush into big decisions.

Mary Beth: I usually recommend that people wait for a year before they rush into any big issues. You never know the dynamics of a family. You can't plan for that. Some heirs may need the money right away, so they might push the executor. Some heirs want to get their share or what's being bequeathed to them now for whatever reason, and that causes stress. As long as someone can encourage the executor that, "Hey, you're in charge. It's on the paper that you're in charge, so you take this at your pace," it makes it easier for everyone involved.

Jess: I like that you say, "To wait a year," because people deal with grief differently. Sometimes, one person will take longer than others, or you go through different stages of grief, and then think you're out of the woods, but you probably aren't. So, waiting a year helps people. Instead of making an emotional or rash decision, waiting allows people to take the time to find out what is right for themselves and their family instead of being forced into making decisions.

That said, what are the main components of estate planning?

Mary Beth: The very, very basics comprise a will, a power of attorney, and a medical power of attorney. Everyone should have these basic ingredients ready because even if you think you don't have an estate, you do. You have money in the bank, or you have a piece of property, or you have a second home or an IRA, a 401(k). Everyone has something of value, and if it's not cared for in the event of something happening, then it can get lost, and that's not what the person might have intended.

Jess: Everyone should have a will, a power of attorney, and a medical power of attorney. How often should they get updated?

Mary Beth: Well, I like to say when there's a life event. Let's say we start out we're in our 20s, we have these things in place, but, now, we've met the spouse of our dreams, and we got married. Well, that's going to change your estate plan. Now we bought a house. Oh, that's going to change it again. Oh, wait. Now we have children. Well, that's going to be a change. Reviewing it with your estate attorney, it's something you should do with a major life change, if you got a divorce or if you had a death in the family, and you've suddenly inherited money. Those are the big key events that would cause you to say, "Hey, maybe I better look at this and see if whatever just happened is covered by my basic will or if I need to update it."

Jess: You have a whole process with estate planning, and I love it because I think it covers two of the areas that are overlooked a lot. Do you mind explaining the four pieces of your estate planning, and how you work with your clients?

Mary Beth: I have put out there that it's called the ESPP process. "E" is the estate plan. That's your power of attorney, your medical power of attorney, your will, and any other documents you might need that your beneficiary will review. That's the dry, necessary piece that you have to do.

My two favorites pieces are sentimental planning and practical planning, and then there's protection planning. All of those components contribute to making a cohesive legacy that you can pass on.

The sentimental planning is probably one of my favorites to manage because anybody can do it at any time. Let's say you have children and they're going off to college. You have saved some of their best artwork and put it in a photo album. It would be labeled like "Johnny did this at age three." "Johnny did this at seven." You might include poetry from seventh grade that you can hand to your child on their way to college, so, they can look back and see their own memories. Or maybe you have everyone in your family write letters to your child on their birthday, and mail them to your home address. You would keep them in a box, and when they went off to college, they can open up the box—and some of those people aren't going to be there anymore. Grandma and Grandpa may not be around by the time Susie goes to college. When Susie opens up her cards, she gets a secure feeling of how much she was loved. Doing this gives kids a good sense of self and purpose as they go out for the first time literally on their own.

Mary Beth: The sentimental piece is only limited by your imagination. Around Christmas, I give my children a Christmas ornament that had to do with whatever they were into that year, whether it was ballet, baseball, whatever. When they moved away for their first time and got their first home, they had a box of ornaments that were only theirs that were given to them. One, they had ornaments, so they didn't have to go out and buy any, and, two, it was like a picture of their lives.

Jess: I love that.

Mary Beth: I have four boxes of ornaments; the older two have theirs, the next one's getting his, and it's really nice because when you visit, you see all those ornaments. It brings back memories for you, as well.

Jess: I think if we sometimes start the estate planning process with the sentimental part, it will help women remember this is why we are doing this planning. We want to remember our loved ones and remember the significant things we've done throughout our lives to help others and to show our love for others. so maybe coming at it-

Mary Beth: Exactly!

Jess: Coming through the process via the sentimental route might be a good first step for women who have been putting off estate planning. They don't want to think about no longer being here, not being able to make decisions for themselves, or their health starting to go.

Mary Beth: I agree with you, but I think any woman listening to this has probably already put in motion without even realizing it that sentimental piece for their children.

They keep a journal. I keep a journal, for instance, and I write a letter to my children on every one of their birthdays. They don't know it, but when I pass away, they'll have all these journals.

Jess: Wow.

Mary Beth: That's what women do. We nurture our children. We want to remember when they were smaller, especially now that my children are getting older. One is married. I still go back to the pictures and just, wow, how quickly that went! I guarantee if you speak to any other mother, they wouldn't think of what they are doing as sentimental planning, per se, but most women have already started.

As women, we unconsciously do it. We teach them grandma's meatball recipe, or we teach them how to bake cookies for Christmas. You're doing it without realizing it in everyday life. You're already doing that sentimental piece.

Jess: I love it. Women are very practical. If I were to leave my daughter with my husband or the babysitter, I'm going to write down every little thing, when she's going to eat, what this sign language means since she can't talk really yet, so she signs. Why don't we do that when it comes to our estate planning?

Mary Beth: Well, I think it's a generational thing, quite frankly.

When you're looking at people 10 years prior to retirement or a few years into retirement—your niche--we're not the computer age. I don't think, "Oh, I should take a picture with my phone." A lot of people in that generation rely on computers like nobody's business. For example, my daughter says to me, "Oh, have you heard of the new motivation for children?" I said, "No, what is that?" She goes, "People change their internet password, and until the chores get done, they don't get the password." That's a foreign concept to me. There was no internet when my kids were being raised. I thought, *boy, that's pretty smart*. If somebody wants to talk to their friends on the phone and they need the Wi-Fi password, they're going to get their chores done.

These are the kinds of thought processes that we don't have. I write down all my usernames and passwords for my husband but there are so many sites that require you to log in, and now every site wants you to one capital, one special character, don't repeat numbers, blah, blah, blah, and it drives you nuts. These are the things that we don't think about.

You may talk to your financial advisor every year, but do they know you have children? Do they know how to reach your children? Are they trying to find out about your children, and vice-versa? Have you spoken to your children about your financial advisor, your CPA, or your estate attorney? Have you given them direction as to who these people are, what you have with them, and what kind of questions they should ask if something happens to you?

The biggest communication failure is, where is all the information?

Is it in one place, or is it scattered all over your desk?

The practical piece is the most important piece that people leave out. I'll share a short story. A coworker passed away, and he had an eight-year-old daughter. His wife came in, and she was fine talking about everything. Then she started crying because she said, "You know, my daughter just wanted to go on the iPad and play a game. She used to play with Daddy, but we didn't have the password."

Jess: Oh, my gosh.

Mary Beth: That's what made her go to tears more than anything else. It's vital that we write these things down, and it's vital that we communicate to the people or person who's going to be in charge. We lock everything, and we lock it with our fingerprint, so we don't even remember what our passwords are.

Jess: It's scary when you don't know where all the pieces are, and it takes so much longer to get settled understanding where you are financially, where everything is, and who to go to. It just prolongs the process so much more, and it doesn't need to be that way. I've been suggesting to people as they come up to retirement that they have those family discussions with the family being present with the advisor, and maybe the estate attorney, and accountant. Then the family can understand what the purpose is, and they can start having a relationship. That way, it's not so scary if they were to lose someone.

Mary Beth: Knowing if you can trust the person that was taking care of your parent, without meeting them, you wouldn't know that. That's a really, really good point, Jess.

Jess: In talking with women in retirement, one of the big fears is that they don't want their kids constantly worrying about them, their health, if they're going to run out of money or if they're making the right decisions. Having those family discussions will help take the worry off the kids, and then the parents worrying the kids are worrying about them.

If you have more than one child, they all have different personalities; they all perceive things differently, and they're all coming from a different place. You can't stop the worry as much as you'd like to. The truth is that's never going to happen, but making preparations is certainly going to make it easier for the person in charge if everything's in one place. If you say to them, "Hey, I have this bright yellow file cabinet, and in it is everything you need to know. It's clearly labeled. That's where you go first if anything happens to me. Inside that file cabinet, you'll find the instructions, who to contact, how to contact them, what information they have, like who has POA, who is the executor, etc., and what you need to do to take care of my affairs."

You need to know where all your insurance policies are. They'll need; your homeowner's insurance, mortgage companies, car insurance, life insurance, etc. The person who's going to take care of your estate needs to know every detail that you know and take for granted.

Jess: You forget how many details they need

If you own a home, you have a business; you have a child, those moving pieces are nothing for you. You know exactly where to go, how to do this, do that, or the other thing. But now someone outside of your routine has to do it. If something happened to me and my husband had to step into what I do, I'm not sure he could without explicit instructions because I just take care of the finances, and that's just the way it falls in my family. To me, it's rote. I know exactly. I have a process. I do it this way, but then he's going to come in and go, "What?"

Mary Beth: You're coming in on somebody else's habit, and it's like trying to teach someone to tie a shoe when they can't look. You're not allowed to look, and you tell me what to do with my hands and these laces so that I can tie a bow on my shoe. If anyone's ever gone through that practice, they know how difficult it is.

It's difficult to walk in your shoes, whether it's your child, your spouse, whoever it might be, your brother, your sister. It's difficult to walk in your shoes and do things for you that you have done for yourself.

Jess: When you don't plan out the practical that we've been stressing on, it leaves a person feeling very vulnerable and scared. It's going to take them so much longer to not only grieve your loss but to get settled into the new life because they're probably going to be wondering, "Is there more money out there? What else could be there? Did I cover everything?"

I remember talking with one widow whose husband passed away from a heart attack unexpectedly. She came to me and said, "I'm terrified of all these what-if scenarios and being blindsided again." She constantly plans out all the different ways that she could be blindsided with her money, with her life, with relationships, and that's not a way to live. You're not going to be able to properly grieve that way because you're always going to be in that survival mode, just trying to get by and trying to get through.

Mary Beth: And you don't want your loved ones to be stuck there.

Jess: That's really when it comes back to what are the priorities? Is it taking some time out of your day now to take care of the practical aspect of it, to save your family all of the fear, the grief, the feeling like the floor's just dropped out from under them? What are you really prioritizing by pushing off building out your estate plan properly?

Mary Beth: I've seen it both ways. I have seen families blow up where siblings never speak to each other again, and I'm sure that their parents are in heaven and crying because that's not what they intended. But you can have all the good intentions in the world, and if you don't put some substance behind your good intentions, it's not going to help your loved ones.

I'm going to make this up, but let's say you're in your 60s and your child is just finishing college, and something happens. They've never had a financial role. They haven't needed one. They're just getting out of college, starting a new job, maybe getting their first apartment, and now they have to take care of your finances? That's a scary thing for someone to get onto that bandwagon, and the learning curve is huge.

If the advisor isn't saying, "Okay. You're 21. You don't know anything, and I'm good with that. I'll walk you through it as many times as you need to hear it. Don't be afraid." It's going to be way more successful than if they have someone talking over their head, and the grief aspect is the most important.

You and I both know this, but the needs of our clients come first. Their emotional well-being is always first. That's why we're passionate about what we do because on my end, dealing with people who are grieving is very difficult. It's terrible. But if you have someone who can nurture their feelings and say, "Listen, we only need to sign here and here. This is what we're going to do. Then we're just going to leave it alone till you're ready," they can breathe. They can take care of the emotional aspects because even if it's a parent who has four kids, every child's going to grieve differently.

It's so important, Jess, that they do the practical part. The sentimental part is the piece that reminds your children how much you loved them and will continue to love them. Our love doesn't stop. It's something tangible that they can validate—the fact that Mom loved me, or Dad loved me. They have the proof of it in their hands. Instead of fighting over the material stuff you left; they have a booklet or ornaments or something that says, "Mom cared about me all these years. She loved me. I know that. I'm rooted, and I'm grounded in that love." This sentimental piece is also a huge part that's going to make getting through the estate process go a little more smoothly. That's huge for their success.

Jess: In our caretaking roles as women, it helps to know we can still take care of our loved ones after we are gone with the extra planning you just described!

Filling in the Gaps in Estate Planning

Getting clear on the purpose estate planning has in your retirement is the first step to filling in the gaps. I'm going to ask you a few questions. Please take a few minutes to think about each one and answer them honestly.

On a scale of 1 to 10, 1 being not very confident and 10 being very confident, answer the following:

1. How confident are you that your money will pass properly to your loved ones? How confident are you that you know how you want your assets to be left?

   1   2   3   4   5   6   7   8   9   10

2. How confident are you that if your health declines, your financial matters will be taken care of the way you want them to and for your benefit?

   1   2   3   4   5   6   7   8   9   10

3. How confident are you that leaving your assets to your family won't cause them any tax implications?

      1   2   3   4   5   6   7   8   9   10

4. How confident are you that your family will be protected financially if something unexpected happened to you?

      1   2   3   4   5   6   7   8   9   10

Your answers give you a starting point for where you stand with your estate plan!

Question 1 deals with the will and beneficiary designations. Your will allows you to dictate where your money goes after you pass away. Beneficiary designations apply to certain types of accounts such as retirement plans (401(k)s, IRAs, annuities, and life insurance policies). A beneficiary designation tells the investment who will inherit the money when you pass away.

Wills should be updated periodically, and especially during times of transition or new events such as weddings, births of children and grandchildren, and changes in wealth. When your children get married, it is time to relook at your will. If you no longer talk with a sibling or loved one, it might be time to rethink their part in your will. Everyone has an estate, no matter how small or big, and so *everyone should have a will.* You might not need the deluxe, luxury will, but having your plan in place will make your heirs so much happier!

Why?

It's not because they no longer have to deal with you, but because it makes settling the estate so much easier.

Question 2 concerns your power of attorney! Let's say you are driving home one day and get into a car accident. You end up in the hospital in a coma and can't make decisions for yourself. Yet, all your bills still need to get paid; your dog needs to get to the vet, and your house needs maintenance. Who will take care of all these for you while you are recovering and mentally getting back to where you were before the accident? The last complication you want is to come back from a health scare to find yourself in an even bigger financial scare! Meet with an estate attorney to create a power of attorney that will cover your real estate, bank accounts, investment accounts, and retirement accounts.

Question 3 brings up the issue that yes, you might know how you want your assets to be left, but don't know if it will cost your heirs more money than necessary. I include this question because it is so important to understand how leaving people money can cost them money! This is why it is crucial to invest time into these documents with the assistance of an estate attorney, the guidance of a financial advisor, and the review of an accountant!

Question 4 covers life insurance and whether there is a need for it in your retirement plan. Some couples love knowing that no matter how much money they spend in retirement, their children, or more likely, grandchildren, are left money. Have you heard of ski-ers? Not the people sliding down the ski slopes BUT the retirees who have titled themselves ski-ers! S-pend K-ids I-nheritance! This is a reality for some families. If not beset by ski-ers, another couple might need life insurance to cover the income from a spouse's pension or income in retirement. When we do a thorough plan for a couple, we always look at three scenarios:

1. What if both spouses live happily ever after?
2. What if one spouse passes early?
3. What if the other spouse passes early?

Trusts

A BIG hot topic now is trusts! Everyone seems to want a trust. They are the new hot handbag of estate planning! But do you really need one, and what are the differences between trusts?

There are living versus testamentary trusts as well as revocable versus irrevocable trusts.

A living trust begins during your life hence the reference to "living"! A testamentary trust starts through your will once you pass away. A revocable trust means you can place assets into the trust and change your mind. An irrevocable trust means you place assets into the trust and cannot change your mind.

Make sense?

A trust can help keep the money you worked so hard for in the family.

One couple in our Strong Retirement Club™ wants to utilize a trust in their estate plans because both of their children are married, and they want to make sure that if the children get divorced, the inheritance stays in the family or in the blood. They also want to ensure the money eventually goes to their grandchildren when they get to a certain age—which they can accomplish through the trust provisions.

A single woman in our Club is using a living trust to help protect against declining health later in retirement. By placing assets into a living trust, she can name a trustee to help pay her bills, manage her money, and make sure she is financially taken care of to her benefit.

There are so many ways to use trusts now, and after you are gone, so I encourage you to get educated, meet with an estate attorney, and bring your advisor along! I love doing family meetings with either the accountant or estate attorney to help ensure everything is working together and in unison!

Here is your estate planning checklist to see what components you have and whether they need to be updated or not!

Check off what you have and explain where you keep it!

_____ Will:

_____

_____ Power of Attorney:

_____

_____ Living Will:

_____

Updates to be made:

_____

_____

_____

_____

_____

Additions to current plan:

Living Trust _____
Testamentary Trust _____
Revocable Trust _____
Irrevocable Trust _____

Executor:

_____

_____

*The executor is responsible for settling your estate, paying the estate's income tax, and passing the money on to the heirs.

Trustee:

_____

_____

*The trustee pays the trust's income taxes, makes sure the trust is being invested prudently for the benefit of the trust beneficiaries, and distributes the money according to the trust provisions to the beneficiaries.

The most beneficial way to dive into estate planning is to do some reflection first. Reflection helps get your thoughts down before you are bombarded with legal jargon! Sit down by yourself, with your partner, or family and go through your top legacy priority.

Here are a few questions to get you started:

Who is your top legacy priority?
What has to happen in your estate plan to make sure your top priority and person are taken care of?
Who can help you accomplish this?

Your estate team can be made up of various professionals such as attorneys, accountants, business coaches (if you own a business), or advisors. I always encourage my Club members to build their DREAM TEAM, or a team of professionals to keep on call for times of planning, crisis, and times of celebration.

As we close this chapter, let me ask you:

Who is on your DREAM TEAM?

Chapter 8: Heir Goes Everything

◊◊◊

"That is your legacy on this earth when you leave this earth: how many hearts you touched."
~Patti Davis

Now that you have the groundwork for an estate plan remember, planning isn't just about the money! How can you show your heirs your money values, and the lessons you've learned, as well as make sure your money, values, and lessons stand the test of time?

By starting now!

If your heirs don't know how much went into building your estate, they might not value it the same way you do.

I've seen it happen a lot!

To put it bluntly... Is someone waiting for you to die?

What I mean by this is: sometimes, when a child knows they are going to inherit wealth, they don't push themselves in their own career. They settle for what is good enough and wait until you die to inherit money to live their life on. Crazy huh? But now that I'm saying it, you probably know at least one person like this! I've even witnessed the heir being unhappy at work, taking it out on their spouse, and still finding no happiness when they do inherit millions. I'm sure this is NOT what you want to happen now or after you are gone.

Start Talking About It

Have a conversation! Begin by talking to your loved ones; share your values of money and of life and connect with them on a different level. You never want the reason you are remembered to be about money. Money and grief do NOT go well together! Too many families break up over money and estate issues, so having the conversation now, and getting everyone on the same page or at least to understand your wishes, will help ensure your money lasts till the end of time. Help instill the values you've lived so they will last well into the future.

I encourage all my clients and club members to have their first family discussion when they retire and enter their Honeymoon. Then, you can explain your estate plan, how you are funding your retirement lifestyle, and be upfront on the expectations of financial gifts now and through your estate. One mom sent her two adult daughters a text right before my meeting with her. It said: "By August I am no longer paying for your car insurance or phone bills."

Their reply: "OK."

Not too bad of a reaction!

We always think this conversation will be worse than it is!

But this mom finally understood that if she is always taking care of everyone else, who will take care of her? The last thing anyone in her family wanted was for Mom to become dependent on her daughters. Her family now supports her goals and retirement wishes and will help keep her accountable for paying off her debt before her retirement deadline!

Once you reach the Relaxation phase of retirement, another very real conversation needs to take place...long-term care. Gather everyone together again to go through your plan, and how it works with your estate plan, then everyone will feel so much more comfortable. If you don't take this step, chances are you will play catch up after a health scare happens. *I do NOT want this for you and your family.* Talk about where all your finances are, and who your attorney, accountant, and advisor are, so your designated people know who to contact to make sure you are taken care of for your benefit if your health starts to go.

Finally, in the Reflection Stage, connect with your loved ones in a meaningful way. Tell them your story. Share with them your lessons, and how they can learn from you to avoid their own regrets. Teach them how to live on their terms now that you've retired on yours. They can apply all that we've gone through together to their lives today! Most of what I've shared with you has been about my life, especially as it pertains to the past year when I've experienced the most personal growth.

I have consciously made an effort to redefine how I live, to start living on my own terms, and to have no regrets. Most of my life, I lived according to other people's expectations of me. It wasn't their fault; it was my own. I didn't know who I was or what I wanted, so I chased what I didn't care about. No wonder I still wasn't happy! I've learned through a lot of soul searching, through great friends and family, and a ton of help, that I can create my own terms to live by. I can live without guilt or regret and still more successful than I was before. By living on my own terms, and redefining my life, I have found a sense of peace and happiness that I am forever grateful for.

So many women come to me to retire, yet they know the typical retirement or the retirement *everyone else wants for them*, just won't do! I know they are the perfect fit for our club because none of us want to live the cookie-cutter life anymore! Our community is all about finding your own path, not the path expected of you, and living your best life. You cannot live your best life without clarity of your values and goals and making sure your money is aligned with both of these factors.

The community gives you the confidence to take back the power of your life, to take back control over your life. This is why we include community, control, and confidence in our logo; they all enhance and support each other. I needed the community to support me during my journey. Being a member gave me the confidence to stand up for my life, and that gave me the power to take back control. That is what our Strong Retirement Club™ is all about, and what our #pinkfix movement revolves around!

Our saying is that for every setback, life struggle, or roadblock, there is a #pinkfix waiting for you!

Grab your #pinkfix and start living your life on your own terms!

Chapter 9: Welcome to the Rest of Your Life

◊◊◊

"She is whatever she wants to be, a little of everything. Mixed up, so tuff in a beautiful way...She has the world at her fingertips because she's a *Strong Woman*."
~ "She Is," Ben Rector, Jeffrey Thomas Pardo

Ready to get lifted up to face what is next in your life? Strong women lift each other up, and I'm ready to help you!

Whether you are facing retirement or not, a new chapter is waiting for you. Are you ready for it?

Do YOU believe there is a next level for your life?

That you can bring your life and those around you to a greater existence, and. A more significant life, where you feel positively challenged? Do you have a positive impact on those around you on a weekly, daily, or hourly basis?

Do you dream to inspire?

Do you dream to live a significant life?

But what does that actually mean? What does that even look like?

If you are CURIOUS, come with me on a journey to unraveling what your life could look like.

Join me, just as you are; no hiding your flaws, trouble spots, or fears. Bring all your money secrets, baggage, and issues. We will need to unwrap each one and put them in a safe place, so you can move forward. The time is now for this journey! Not tomorrow, or "maybe one day," but TODAY. If you don't find the time now to rediscover yourself, will you ever find the time?

The BIG secret is that there is NO perfect moment to start this journey.

You can't wait until you hit a certain salary, amount in your savings, or get through a rough patch in your life. There is no magical time to begin; the best time to begin is NOW! Find out how to get started by taking our quick *QUIZ*!

E-book readers, you will find the hyperlink easy to access. All other readers, please go here to take your quiz: www.jessicaweaver.com/moneybaggage

After you take the quiz, read through Lisa Chastain's Finding and Loving Your New Identity interview below to learn what there is to adore about this stage of refinement:

Meet Lisa!

Lisa is a money coach from Las Vegas, Nevada who typically works with millennial women who make good money but have little to show for it. She is a #1 Best Selling Author of Girl Get Your $hit Together, a speaker, and a powerhouse! Lisa is my accountability buddy, and together, we have been through some of the toughest times as well as the happiest times. Lisa has been a guest speaker in our Strong Retirement Club™. She has also been featured in our Money Workshops. Her work leaves an impact and inspires you to tap into a new will to level up your life. Join Lisa and me as we dive into what identifies us as humans, as women, and as new retirees.

Jess: I'm excited to talk with you today about living our most authentic lives, and what that means. We tend to be so tied to our careers. Our identity is so tied to what we do for a living, but in retirement, we don't have that anchor anymore. What I've noticed is a lot of women are lost as to their purpose is in retirement, and when we're lost and we don't know what direction we're going in, we get pulled in different directions. Then we spend money on things that we don't really care about. Which brings me to this question: What does living authentically mean to you?

Lisa: So we all have dreams. And if we go back to our earliest memories of being young, as little girls dreaming and playing, there's this spirit inside of us. I truly believe we were all born with a purpose and a destiny. But our connection to that gets lost over time because we get stuck working, in a routine; we get attached to other people. A lot of women have children and grandchildren, and we attach our identities to being mothers and grandmothers. If we were to take the time to dream again, I believe that women and anyone really if they have the time to center and focus, will connect to their higher purpose in life.

To get reconnected, consider these questions: What are you here for? What is your ultimate why in life?

Remember, when we lose sight of our purpose, we feel out of control. We feel out of balance. Maybe we feel depressed.

Living our authentic lives means taking action, and making decisions, ultimately in the direction of our destiny every single day. A lot of people have high-value systems, so for them, it might mean reintegrating and realigning into what we value. It could be family, or spiritual, our connection to God. We are talking about taking your life to a higher level and becoming a more self-actualized person, so when we die, we can say we did what we came here to do. Living authentically can mean living in connection with our values, but it also means honoring our higher calling and purpose in life.

Jess: Do we just not have the time to think about what our calling is? Or do we distract ourselves? Maybe the callings scare us? Or intimidate us?

Lisa: A lot of the women that I work with have huge dreams. Once they realize what it's going to take to make those dreams come true, fear steps in. A lot of women will use the language of, "I don't know how." Or, "It sounds too difficult."

In the world of work, in the masculine sense, a lot of our value is placed on what we do but living authentically has so much more to do with *the kind of women we see ourselves being in the world*. Mother Theresa is a great example of this. Although her work in Calcutta was life-altering, it was who she was being for those people that summoned her to the higher purpose and calling in her life. So I think it's more that we don't take the time to reflect and especially in the hustle and bustle of raising kids and working and building careers, we don't take time to ask the right questions. It's most important to ask the right questions of ourselves to call us forward.

I spoke about this in the Retirement Club; this is the last great chapter of their lives. It is ultimately an opportunity to rewrite the script, to lay it all out on the line, and if women, in particular, don't take the time to stop and ask deeper more thoughtful questions about what they want the rest of their lives to look like, it's a lost opportunity.

Jess: I've seen women floundering along in retirement. They thought they'd figure it out in the first few months, but then a few months turned into a year. That year turns into a few years, and then they come to me and say, "I'm bored. I don't know what to do, so I sit at home, terrified to do anything because I am going to run out of money, or my health is going to fail me."

Through the club, we talk about the three stages of retirement, the Honeymoon, Relaxation, and Reflection stages. We start with the Honeymoon where everything is fun; you're loving life and traveling, doing all kinds of things. In the relaxation stage, you slow down a little. Sure, you're still doing things, but you can sleep in, get up when you want to, and spend more time with family and friends.

But then the reflection stage begins, and this is when we finally take the time to look at how authentic has our life been. What has the significance of our life been for those around us? And that's why, when you've lived your authentic life, as you say, it makes it so much easier to move into that reflection stage. It makes it so much easier to come to terms with death, too, with not being here any longer. When you have lived authentically, you know you've made your impact on the world that you are supposed to.

Lisa: Wouldn't that be the ideal that everybody could have that experience as they wind down, as their bodies age. They could have more time to reflect and look back. They could be really proud of themselves. Yes, that would be ideal.

Jess: Then, even if they have regrets, they can make good on those regrets. They can fix what they need to. We're all going to have regrets in life, but it's what you do after reflecting on those regrets that matters.

And how does living authentically work with our money? Do we do certain things with our money based on how we live as a person?

Lisa: Every choice we make in our life always comes back to having some type of financial consequence, repercussion, or reward. So if someone's in their 50s, looking at what the rest of their life is going to be like, the decision she's making today will have financial consequences one way or the other. We can't do anything in this world without spending money. This is why it's so stressful to think about retirement. I'm in my late 30's, and when I think about it, I get overwhelmed and wonder, *oh my God, am I going to have enough money*? I can only imagine the stress level of someone in their 50s or early 60s who doesn't have clarity. Because it stops us.

Without the clarity that you're going to have enough, you need to be able to answer what is enough and what do you need it for?

Your answer shouldn't just concern your household expenses and make the minimums are met. But I would imagine so many of the women that you work with have had dreams of what they want to actually experience in retirement, that they didn't get the opportunity to do as a working woman, or when they were raising children or supporting their husband or whatever else took up her time in her life.

It all comes back to looking at your finances and asking how it will support you in having the experiences, making the memories, and giving back, rather than making sure that the lights stay on.

Jess: You don't want to just pay your bills and then die. That's not what it's about either. These women have very big bucket lists when they come up to retirement because they just didn't have time to what they've wanted to do all their lives. We determine what are the top priorities? What are the top goals? What do they really want? Then critically, what is the dollar amount associated with each one of those plans? When we help them arrive at the answers to these questions, they can figure out *is this what I really want? Do I want to put all this money toward one bucket list item? Or is there something else I want to do with it that, is more aligned with how I want to live my life in retirement*?

It's interesting because you work with millennial women or women who make good money, but they don't really have much to show for it. They're stuck in that hustle and bustle. Do you see them having similar issues to women near and in retirement?

Lisa: I do when it comes to clarity. I work with couples and single women, and even if they don't have a ton of debt, they don't have any money in savings because they have not made intentional choices with their money. They've been listening to subconscious thoughts their parents told them growing up. These are assumptions they believe about money. The work that I do with millennial women is the same work that I would do with the pre-retiree.

For example, I have a client who's desperate to retire. She is so ready to retire, and she has no idea how to even answer the question if she can retire. You've probably experienced where women come to you, and they urge you, "Just tell me yes or no." But it's so much more complicated. This is similar to the question I hear from both millennial women and women in their 40's: Can I afford this career change? Can I afford this house? Can I afford this trip?

Jess: It's not that simple.

Lisa: No, you need to know; are you living a purposeful life? And why does this stuff matter in the first place? Those are the tougher questions to answer that we need to get to work on as soon as possible. We ask those questions in the first meetings I have. And I do believe it causes some frustration out of the gate because they these women want a simple answer. But there is no simple answer because there are a lot of questions first that need answering. The goal is to design a life instead of just getting by.

Jess: Giving them a simple answer isn't fixing the real problem either. It's just going to put a temporary fix on it and give them false hope. Some of the women we talk to, feel like *I got your answer, now I can do it on my own*. We both know managing any of this planning on your own is very, very hard to do.

Lisa: Simply saving for retirement is not an acceptable answer either. Just because you have money saved for retirement, doesn't mean it's going to be a great retirement if you don't have your spending under control—if you aren't living with intention.

Jess: That's why you have to learn how you want to live, and then you can make the money correlate. You want to work in the same direction, so you're not constantly fighting against yourself. We can revert back to how we define a successful life. Or success. Women near retirement and reaching that level of success might have been defined by how far in their career they went, how much money they saved, or how much money they earned. But that's stripped away in retirement. I can see women who are coming into the workforce or shifting jobs with the same problem. They might think *I have this nice, high paying job but I hate it*. The paycheck pulls them back into their occupation, but it's not making them happy because their vision of success has changed.

What's going to give them satisfaction has changed.

This process requires thought and deliberate actions.

It requires having someone in your life ask the right questions and guide you. This isn't necessarily going to happen on its own.

Jess: It's not going to be an overnight change, and sometimes you need somebody to guide you and to give you permission to invest in yourself. Sometimes, you need the go-ahead to invest the money, and time, and to go through the process to save them time and money years down the road.

Lisa: That's the big message to the younger women I work with. Even if you spent six months to a year on these things, you would be better off in the long run.

Jess: What do they say, spend money to make money, but you have to invest time to gain time back.

And if you're going to do it, you might as well do it right. You might as well execute it properly and not just half-ass it or try to DIY it.

Do it right if you're going to spend the time doing it.

Lisa: I agree.

Jess: Do you want to talk about your Girl Get Your $hit Together Academy?

Lisa: My hope is that this is a program young women around the world can identify as a place to come and get to work on building a purposeful life, and a life with intention. Here, they can align their money choices with what they really want. It's a year-long program, and women spend three weekends working on themselves. I believe that the best investment a woman can make is investing in herself and making sure that she has the confidence and clarity not only with her money but in her career, in ensuring her relationships are fully aligned with who she is in life. So, I designed a program that allows them to start as soon as possible learning how to best manage their money, and from there, learning about money period. Because it's an entirely new language. I know; I spent years learning the language of money. There's a learning curve.

These women come in with very little knowledge, other than the fact that they know how to earn money and have an opportunity for a year to invest in themselves. When they do this, their financial future is bright. They're making choices in the direction of their dreams and not just haphazardly. They're making wise choices for their future.

Jess: Yeah, one of our members, Kirsten, always asks her clients, "If you are an investor and had $100,000 to invest in one person and her ideas, would you invest in yourself?" That's a really interesting question. Then we have to think, *if the answer is no, what has to happen to believe in yourself enough to invest money in yourself?*

Lisa: Your first book, *Strong Woman, Stronger Assets*, well, I'm working on the stronger woman part of that equation. I do have a lot of women who come in, who haven't had a mentor. To them, I say, "I believe in you. You can do this." Not only are they creating amazing financial results in their lives, but they're really leveling up in life. Their health is better; they're eliminating toxic relationships; they're transforming relationships, and they're getting to know themselves on a deeper level. That is worth its weight in gold.

Jess: Once you take a stand for your life, it's amazing where you're going to go. Like you said, you make better choices for your own life in all different areas. Relationship, health, money, learning, education-

Lisa: Career.

Jess: And you probably see this too, but you usually inspire the ones around you to do the same.

Lisa: Yes, you can.

Jess: But it's not immediate. Sometimes these women will rebel against it until suddenly, they start thinking the same way.

Lisa: They will, or they won't. The ones who will, see you and hang with you differently. The ones who don't go their own direction and that's perfectly normal and okay.

I had to walk away from a marriage. It just wasn't serving me at the highest level, and we don't have a toxic relationship today. So, that's one example of how fear steps in for a lot of women. They may have big dreams, but they're afraid of losing people or afraid of change. Being different with your money means you may need to be different about your life. And that may not work for some people in your life. That fear holds us into relationships, careers, or health. We don't know what we don't know. Still have the courage to start asking questions and find the right people, like you and me and our programs. Find other women who are doing the same work, and there you'll find courage, even if you can't do it on your own at first.

Jess: Just take that one little risk to reach out for help, that one little stretch because it's going to be risky, it's going to be uncomfortable. But that usually needs to happen to get at the real change women are looking for.

Lisa: I believe in the heart of hearts when we take the time to be still and listen to ourselves, we know what's working and what's not working. Maybe a woman reading your book right now can discover the courage to listen to herself, and then she'll begin to answer her own questions. There are ways to guide people through that as well but start by listening to your hearts and making choices aligned in that direction. That's the path to authenticity.

Jess: What a lovely message, to be still; because we hate being still.

We busy ourselves to death, but there is something so powerful about being still and silent and in the moment.

To take time, ask yourself the hard questions, and feel out your emotions with each answer.

Beginning Our Journey

As we start our journey together, I want you to think back to the scariest time you had with your money. This was a moment when you felt vulnerable, insecure, and in such a state of fear. Can you think of it? Picture it and feel your emotions. I know it's not fun. But going there is so necessary, so you can make a commitment right now to NEVER let a moment like that happen again. You are taking the first step to becoming accountable to stop living in survival mode, to live comfortably with your money and life.

Moving from SURVIVAL mode to COMFORTABLE starts with your mind. When you get stuck on the hamster wheel, it is so hard to get off because you really feel you don't have the time to even think about anything else. You're so busy, right?

I get it.

So, make the time right now. Take a few minutes and write down all the thoughts that arise when you think about money. How many are negative, and how many are positive? Rewrite all your negative ones and make them positive. This is a great first step to rewriting your Money Mantra, which is what we call it in my book: "Strong Woman Stronger Assets."

Moving into Success

If you feel COMFORTABLE with your money now, then how do you move to the SUCCESS level? Staying at a comfortable level is one of the riskiest AND easiest things to do. This is because you get so comfortable being well, comfortable! It's convenient, familiar, and allows you to get so complacent with your life. Now is the time to reach out for help to someone who will push you and challenge you in a positive way. To reach success, you have to be ready to get uncomfortable, so uncomfortable that you want to go back to that nice and cozy comfortable level. You'll want to go back so badly that you'll need someone to hold you accountable to keep reaching and stretching and pushing forward.

My business coach, Robyn Crane, did just this when I hired her to work with me. I've lived the most uncomfortable years since I met her, but I wouldn't change any of it! If she hadn't been there pushing me, my book wouldn't be published, my *Strong Retirement Club™* would never have been created, and I would not be living my best life. Who will push you and hold you accountable? You can choose the same person or two different people!

I will push you, and together we will hold each other accountable, so I'm serving you with my best, and you are implementing what I give you. When we work together, we both execute YOUR plan together to move you beyond the SUCCESS level and right up to the SIGNIFICANT level in YOUR life!

Welcome to the Most Significant Level of Your Life

Congratulations, you are now entering the most life-changing phase of your life...the SIGNIFICANT phase. This is my favorite of all the stages because, in this step, your plan goes from being about YOU to being about all of those around you. We center on YOUR impact on the world around you! I'm not working with you to just *help you*; I want to work with you to help everyone around you: your family, loved ones, and even your own clients. Take a moment and pause in your busy life. Ask yourself: are you living your purpose? Are you doing what God put you on this Earth to do? What type of impact do you have on people around every day? If you're ready to make a REAL impact, a lasting impact beyond your life, it's time to get serious and talk!

I invite you to find out how our Strong Retirement Club™ (http://bit.ly/TheRetirementSuiteGroup) can help answer these questions while you enjoy the guidance, knowledge, and support needed to make a LASTING impact!

Are you curious yet? Want to know more about our community? Do you think there is another level for your life?

Are you ready to bring your life to the next level?

To open up and find how to bring your life to the next level, you need to detox your brain. You need to quiet your mind, stop any haphazard thinking, and turn off all the distractions around you. When you do this, take notice of your thought patterns. Which ones bring you stress? Which ones get you excited? Which ones bring you joy and comfort?

You'll also notice the thoughts you keep getting stuck are preventing you from digging deeper. You could be hanging up on a deep, dark fear, a really sad memory, or an area you aren't allowing yourself to explore. Why do you keep getting stuck on these thoughts? What is blocking you from going deeper? Usually, these thoughts are holding you back.

Write down the thoughts you are getting stuck on and what emotions they bring up.

1._____

2._____

3._____

You have the power to accept a thought or not, and by recognizing these thoughts, you can now decide which to keep and which to discard. Are these thoughts helping you achieve your retirement dreams or preventing you from attaining them? As you complete this activity, you might recognize the negative and positive patterns in your thinking. Humans are created to think positively, but you might have been brought up with negative parents, teachers, or even have a negative spouse in your life, which has led you to thinking more negatively.

I call it the SPIRAL!

One negative thought snowballs into ruining your entire day, your mindset, and your attitude. You end the day feeling horrible! This happened to me a lot while I was dealing with postpartum depression. I've noticed it with a lot of retirees as well, especially if their spouse or family members keep telling them they should have kept working or that they'll run out of money.

When they hear such thoughts brought to life, it leaves people paralyzed to do anything. So, they don't leave the house, and they are terrified to spend more. A new retiree told me she sits on the couch all day because her husband chirps in her ear every morning that they'll run out of money.

Is this reality?

NO!

We've done the planning numerous times, and this couple was on track to be better than fine with their money. But when you hear the opposite every day; you start to believe it and even trust it.

The problem with negative thinking is that creates what you expect from your retirement. Your negative thinking creates negative realities! The good news is positive thoughts create positive expectations, which bring you positive realities!

Negative thinking isn't natural for us, which is why it doesn't feel good to think negatively.

Doing this exercise to detox your brain is so important. It shows you who is influencing you, and what triggers your negative thinking.

What are your triggers when it comes to your money and negative thinking or emotions?

What are your triggers when you get stuck on a thought, and can't go any deeper?

Learning about your triggers is essential in helping you create positive thinking, positive attitudes, and positive realities in your retirement!

Let's hear them! What are your triggers?

1. _____

_____

2. _____

_____

3. _____

_____

Linda is a woman in her 70s who was still working but dealing with health issues. She LOVED her job, but her health was making it harder and harder each day to stay at work. She had an inner conflict going on because of her love for work but felt the need to slow down to take care of herself. Another issue that kept coming into play was her children. One child would tell her to keep working so she wouldn't be bored at home once she retired. The other child told her to retire and move to the beach. How could she win with both children telling her something different? Her fear of being bored at home, her fear of running out of money, and her fear of her not having her health to travel in retirement were all triggers.

Her reaction to her triggers was to avoid them! We all have different reactions to our triggers; some triggers will push you to work harder while others might turn you into a deer in headlights. Learning about your triggers and how you respond will help you get unstuck and level up your life.

In Linda's case, I had to get her to open up and stop avoiding the topic. It was easier to have these tough conversations over lunch and talk through each decision she would have to make to see what the outcomes would be. Doing this gave her the confidence to understand how each choice would impact her not just tomorrow but in 10 or 20 years. This new knowledge provided her the security of knowing she had me on her team to always come back to when a trigger was set off. It gave her the control to find the right choice for her right now even if her plan were to change down the road. She now had clarity over the direction of her new life. Going this deep and exploring her triggers gave her the trust she needed to retire and find a different way to live on her terms without any regrets!

The way you think is so powerful! It can change your genetic expression and constantly restructure your brain. (Sorry, had to get geeky with you!)

If you think about it, you have the power to change your thinking, whether you want to accept a thought as real or not. When you were growing up, you were put in a box, and that box became your self-worth. I am here today to let you know, you can NOW take yourself out of the box, and not let the box limit you anymore. If you want more on how to change your self-worth, check out my first book *Strong Woman Stronger Assets*, to learn how to raise your self-worth to gain total control, clarity, and confidence in your money.

"Today you are YOU, that is truer than TRUE. There is no one alive who is YOUER than YOU!" Dr. Seuss

So, who are YOU? Who are you now that you aren't stuck in a box?

Let's take a moment to do a reflection exercise. Grab your journal or use the space below to write a letter to yourself. As you write the letter, reflect on these questions:

1. Who do you want to be in your life right now?
2. Who do you want to be in your retirement?
3. What does that person look like, feel like, dress like?

Imagine you are a NEW person. You are no longer the person your parents, spouse, friends/boss/co-workers wanted you to be. You are just YOU, so who is that person?

1. What drives you?
2. What makes you feel loved?
3. What gives you purpose each day?

Chapter 10: In Parting

◊◊◊

"If you don't design your own life, chances are you'll fall into
someone else's plan. And guess what they have planned for you?
Not Much!"
~Jim Rohn

What does retiring on your own terms mean? Now that you have read through the book, I hope you have a better understanding of how you want to retire. You probably have been living your life according to everyone else's standards, society's standards, and what has become your normal. But have you ever thought where those standards came from? Who started them, who kept them going, who reinforced them? You've been living a certain way because of what others have told you to do, whether it was your parents, peers, boss, or what you've read, or heard. Scary, isn't it?

Think about your money.

You've been saving a certain way, spending a certain way, and managing your money a certain way because of what others have told you to do. In the end, do you really know if the choices you have made are what is best for your money?

My goal is for you to strip away all the standards, expectations, and ways you might regard living in retirement and start fresh! Build a brand-new way to live.

Remember, it is TIME TO REFINE your life and live on your own terms.

Not the terms set by anyone before you!

I've heard from so many women whose family says: "Don't retire, you'll be bored at home!" Or "You should retire and enjoy your life. Forget about work!" Or "Don't move away. We'll never see you." Or "Move away, you don't want to stay and be bored at home."

It's understandable that you would feel like you are being pulled in so many directions, hoping you won't disappoint anyone and terrified you'll let everyone down. All these feelings leave you in a state of guilt. Guilt is a scary emotion; it is an exhausting and harmful feeling. It leads to injury and illness and can paralyze you. You become so hard on yourself from these feelings of guilt that you start to doubt yourself. That self-doubt can cripple your future.

When you start doubting yourself, you spiral downward. Anytime you hear something that reinforces your doubt, you spiral even lower. As my therapist says: "CUT THE CHAIN! Stop the spiral by stopping the self-doubt by stopping the guilt!"

I know this feeling all too well. I've been in a family business for the past nine years; it's all I've ever known in my career. A few years ago, I started the women's division of our firm offering services and new programs along with my blog: Not Your Father's Advisor, my book *Strong Woman Stronger Assets*, my workshops and speaking engagements/appearances, my Strong Retirement Club™, and now this book. I wasn't following the traditional method of financial planning because it doesn't work for people, gives them false hope, and isn't sustainable. I wanted the women I work with to experience real change and a real impact on their lives. I wanted to help transform how they live.

I tossed the training book out, rewrote the script, and found a new way to give the women I work with even more help.

This service hits a whole new level with a community for support and encouragement, various professionals on-call to help, and a path to make lasting change in lives. So, even if you are already working with an advisor, I invite you to check out our community to see how we can complement what you are currently doing or find a better way to manage your money, or multi-task it to ease your life. My perspective isn't necessarily better, but it is different and brings fresh new energy into your retirement.

Because it is so different, I had some doubts early on, but I also saw the transformation it brought. My mind would always want to come back to the traditional way of doing things, and any time I'd hear someone try to belittle or downplay my work, I believed them. When this happens, you develop an inner conflict that leaves you exhausted, and for me, sick. I spent the past year sick with different colds and infections as well as weeks of neck spasms. I finally realized the real issue wasn't my daughter being in daycare or my poor posture.

It was the guilt!

I had guilt that I wasn't living up to everyone else's expectations of me and my work.

Guilt can do a lot of harm to you, so before we end our journey together, think about what guilt you are living with right now. Journal about it and see what justification the guilt has in your life. Should it be there? Probably not. When you let go of everyone else's expectations of your life and retirement, you will set yourself free of the guilt. This is my commitment to you.

Now that you are FREE, you need to hear that you were always STRONG. Even if you need to be reminded every now and then (why do you think I wear my strong bracelet every day!), let yourself believe it as you prepare to live on your own terms!
Please use this book to build out how you want to live in retirement now that you have the understanding, information, beliefs, and finally the trust that you can do it, throw out all the expectations

and standards of how you should live. It's time to find YOUR way to live. It's time to retire on your own terms, not anyone else's!

To my strong ladies out there,

"Your life is too short, to not live on your own terms,
Your business is too important, to not work on your own terms,
You're too special, to not live on your own terms,
You are too strong, to not live on your own terms, and it's

Time to refine...your life and live on your own terms."

With love,
Jess

References/Bibliography

1. "Weighing the Costs and Need for Long-term Care Insurance - Part 1." WTOP. August 08, 2018. Accessed June 01, 2019. https://wtop.com/business-finance/2018/08/weighing-the-costs-and-need-for-long-term-care-insurance-part-1/.

About the Author

Meet Jess!

I'm thrilled to "meet" you and be on this journey with you. Do you want my boring bio or the #pinkfix one?

I want to help you in any way that fits into your world. We have different channels to bring you into our world whether it is to read my blog: Not Your Father's Advisor every week, pick up my books when you need an inspiring message, be a one on one client of mine, or be a member in our Strong Retirement Club™. However you fit into our community, we are thrilled to have you and grateful to support you!

About Jess:

Jessica Weaver, CFP®, CDFA™, CFS® is a Wealth Advisor, who focuses her work on women like YOU!

Jess found herself on a mission to help more women gain control, clarity, and confidence over their finances and the next chapter of their life. Her focus is on women nearing retirement or in retirement to help guide them through their money concerns, questions, and emotions. Most of the women Jess works with have done a good job-saving money but are missing the link to creating a retirement income from it.

"In retirement, every dollar needs to have its purpose and to maximize every opportunity out there." ~**Jessica Weaver.**

After witnessing both of her grandmother's struggle with retirement, running out of money, and dealing with the aftermath of their estates, Jess knew she had to take a stance. She began running workshops and events to help women gain control over their money before it was too late. In 2018, Jess founded the Strong Retirement Club™ to fix the increasing issue most women in retirement face...their lack of trust. She wants every woman who comes into her world to gain trust in themselves to live their fullest life without any regrets.

Jess has been on this mission since 2015 when she founded the Women's Division of her firm's branch. She started hosting events for women as she began building this community to help, guide, and encourage women, which led to the start of her blog: Not Your Father's Advisor. After Jess saw the increasing views to her popular blog, she knew there was a bigger need to make a topic like money more approachable for women. In 2017, Jess decided to write her #1 Best Selling book: *Strong Woman Stronger Assets*, while pregnant with her first daughter.

Through her online presence, public speaking, blog, her book, and her Strong Retirement Club™, she is able to touch more lives than she ever thought possible and help them elevate their life to the next level. She is incredibly grateful for the opportunity to be a part of your life and to help with your own transformation.

"It is my life mission to educate, encourage, and transform women's lives. And maybe have some fun along the way." ~Jessica Weaver

She welcomes you into her #pinkfix world at: www.jessicaweaver.com where you can read her blog: Not Your Father's Advisor, join her next workshop, watch her show series, or see Jess speak as well as grab Jess's first #1 best-selling book *Strong Woman Stronger Assets.*

If you are curious about Jess's Strong Retirement Club™, you can learn about the membership at www.strongretirementclub.com. She'd love to talk with you about your own retirement and how a community atmosphere can bring a new level of preparation to your goals. Throughout the year, Jess hosts retirement focused roundtables, workshops, and retreats to help you refine your life.

And there's MORE to come!

#pinkfix Productions is a new line for Jess's blog, where her books, details on workshops, and media are located. National #pinkfix Day is May 17th, which we will be celebrating with women around the United States each year. You can join Jess's #pinkfix movement by following Jess on Facebook at: https://www.facebook.com/jessica.claire.7965 and on Instagram at https://www.instagram.com/jessweaver4/ and apply to be a #pinkfix ambassador in your area!

Want to know more about our community? Check out our Business Plan Summary!

Business Plan
Jessica Weaver

Company's Values:

- Educate women above all else!
- Support other female business owners.

- God first, family second, community third...that is just how we roll!
- Always show women our excitement, love, and gratitude for working with them.
- Help women live their best lives by committing to their goals with them.
- Embrace innovation!
- Be compassionate because we don't know where someone else is coming from. Never judge.
- Maintain vision and integrity with every opportunity.

Company's Culture:

- There is always a #pinkfix behind any dark cloud, bumpy road, or tough time.
- Always celebrate the women in our community, their successes, and our anniversaries together.
- Start each event by popping a cork!
- Community, confidence, control.
- Maintain passion, fun, and enjoyment with each task.
- Community of safety and trust.

Executive Summary:

We are here to help and support women with their money first and with their lives second. We will always educate women in regards to their finances and money decisions by giving them the information they need, help them understand the information, build their beliefs in themselves, and the trust that they can do it. Our community is here to bring women together who are going through a similar time in their lives, to give them confidence with their money, and control over their lives. We do this through our events and workshops, club membership, and by supporting other female business owners.

BOOK MY CALL with JESS!
(www.jessicaweaver.setmore.com)

#pinkfix Productions Presents

◊◊◊

#pinkfix Powerbooks: Leveraging Your Feminine Empowerment at Every Age and Stage!

I've been hard at work on my latest book, *Time to Refine, which is a deep dive* into the world of retirement. But before you can even think about retirement, you need to get a grasp on your relationship with money and the role it's playing in your life. *Strong Woman Stronger Assets, How to Raise Your Self Worth to Raise Your Net Worth to Help Gain Total Control, Clarity, and Confidence with Your Money* explains the essential foundation needed to build upon, so you can grow your money just like a garden with many layers. In your garden, you need the right soil, level ground, and shade and sun areas before you can add your beautiful flowers. I'm ready to help you dig into your dream garden, smooth out the rough edges, unearth the rocks and boulders and nurture the pretty pink flowers that will bloom for years to come.

Your refinement garden comes to be as a result of pinpointing your value and assets—which is the premise of my first book.

The # 1 best-selling, *Strong Woman Stronger Assets, How to Raise Your Self Worth to Raise Your Net Worth to Help Gain Total Control, Clarity, and Confidence with Your Money* is book one of the *#pinkfix Powerbooks* that instruct you in capitalizing on your true value in life, how to better negotiate that value, and how to leverage your power to raise your net worth. It is the perfect companion to *Time to Refine.*

My mission in life is to reach as many women as possible to help them take control of their money no matter the challenges they face. After experiencing the relief and joy of simple and blissful money management, I know you'll agree there is no other way to live!

I'm here to tell you; money doesn't need to control your life anymore. In writing about my money story and sharing numerous other stories in my books, I am touching so many more lives than I ever dreamed. These books are the highlights of my years of experience, learning, and successes that I hope you will use to help you navigate the many questions you may have about your money. I've dedicated my weekends and late nights to writing these #pinkfix Powerbooks just for you. You can end the haphazard money management habits we have all been guilty of practicing— sometimes, just because we never learned a better way!

It's time to change that reality and look through a different lens, one where you are empowered to make your soundest financial and life decisions.

Prepare to tap into the magic of living your self-worth. Being "stuck" or "trapped" in your current life, means you are accepting NOT living up to your self-worth. But you can change your financial and life trajectory drastically by making small changes with your money, and in how you behave with your money... Money impacts every aspect of your life, whether you want to admit it or not. In *Strong Woman Stronger Assets*, you will discover how your relationship with money may be jeopardizing your future; how to modify your current money beliefs and behaviors to enhance your goals, and how to build your new plan, and identify what "asset" you are working for.

What you most want in life doesn't come down to money. More money isn't going to fix your financial issues. Let me help you find your unique happiness to put yourself on a path to get more enjoyment out of your life.

Once you embrace your path to more meaningful living in every area of your existence, you'll be ready to strategize your retirement to your greatest advantage. The one thing I know about retirement is this: any fears or concerns you have about money now, only get multiplied once that paycheck stops coming in. What you thought was your safety net of regular income is gone, and now it is on you to recreate it, which will bring out insecurities you've been avoiding with your money. I want you to live your life with purpose without your money fears haunting you around every corner, looming over every good moment, and slamming into you while you are down. When you are ready to commit to living a life without regret, without fear holding you back, then you are ready for your own #pinkfix Powerbooks! From your first paycheck to your last wish of refinement, I've got you covered with our NEW, pinked-out book series!

After writing *Strong Woman Stronger Assets* and now *Time to Refine*, you're probably wondering, "what's next?"

A guidebook on building your Queendom, of course!

Money Empire, a Strong Woman's Guide to Creating Her Own Money Queendom is my next brainchild, and one I know you need to ensure what you have learned in the first two #pinkfix Powerbooks keeps paying out!

Money Empire was inspired because every strong woman needs an empire to fund her BIGGEST dreams! These are dreams only strong women dare to dream. It's time to run your money like you run your business. After all, this is the business of your life...funding your life.

It's time to stop imitating how men create and manage wealth, too, and do it our way. As you know...the future is female! Always working harder, and hitting the pavement as men have done for ages, is only going to cause you burnout. A woman's way needs to work on her schedule, fit in between time with family, building a career, and having cocktails with her girlfriends. This is why my next mission is to hand you the bricks to build your Money Empire that will shield you from being fried and frustrated from always working harder but not getting anywhere—all from being exhausted because progress takes too damn long.

Building your Money Empire requires commitment, guidance, and focus. But don't worry mama, you have all three; you just need to stay committed and focused!

We both know that is where you shine.

You should also know to feel fully confident in your money decisions, especially as it pertains to investing, you need to understand the consequences of your decisions. Ask yourself: *How will this investment affect me not just tomorrow, but years down the road?* What will this investment cost me to make more money? How long will it take? And how much do I have to risk to be rewarded?

The missing piece, and arguably, the biggest piece to identify is *what purpose does this investment have in my portfolio? Is it bringing income, building gains, or giving me tax benefits*?

You don't just want to throw together a portfolio or put your money into an investment. Think about the intention behind your choices. Will they help with long-term care costs? Will they protect your heirs if you pass away? Will they give you guaranteed income for life? If there is no purpose, you will feel insecure about the investment. Prioritize your needs for investing; identify your weak areas, and find investments that address these aims. Then you will understand why you should or should not add investments to your portfolio mix! When you are clear about your money's purpose, it gives you confidence in your decisions! You will learn how to build your own Money Empire and position your money to pull in different streams of income. After implementing my money strategies, your every dollar will be accounted for and given purpose. This is YOUR opportunity to grow, and your opportunity to give yourself financial liberation! It's a feeling even better than taking off your bra at the end of a very long day!

You might have questions about creating your Money Empire, and I am here to answer them so you can leverage your financial edge.

You might be wondering...

What does it take to build a Money Empire? What does a Money Empire even look like? In your next journey with me, we will go through the key items to build, manage, and rule your Money

Empire. In fact, my goal for you in *Money Empire* is to learn that your life is worth the BIG dreams. Why not you? Why not now?

Here's what we'll cover on your road to ruling your Queendom!

- Building a money plan like you would a business plan that will grow as you grow—allowing your dreams to become MASSIVE!
- Creating multiple streams of income to fund <u>your business of living</u>.
- Identifying every dollar coming into your life, where it's coming from, and the cost to acquire it. Conditioning yourself to become more efficient to avoid burnout as you grow your empire.
- Implementing structure in your investments, giving your investments purpose, and composing your money laws to live by.
- How to manage your money manager, money council, and money partners.
- Letting yourself reign as your own Money Queen as you go after your <u>Big Girl Dreams</u>!

You're not merely building a financial plan...you're constructing a Money Empire, and it's your turn to rule your Queendom! No one else can do it for you!

#pinkfix Powerbooks is a series of manuals for the modern woman's life to be used at every stage and age.

Strong Woman Stronger Assets exposes your love-hate relationship with money to find out why you act in certain ways. You'll learn how to implement small, easy changes in your day-to-day life to make drastic transformations in your finances. (Find the book here: http://bit.ly/StrongWomanStrongerAssets)

Time to Refine is the next level and book in the #pinkfix Powerbooks. Read it and practice living life on your terms. Once you have mastered your money, then you've taken the steps to reach book three...

Money Empire provides you with every tool you need to construct your empire. After all, every strong woman needs one!

#pinkfix Powerbooks: Leveraging Your Feminine Empowerment at Every Age and Stage!

Let me help you unlock your divine female power to own every aspect of your world.

All you have to do is turn the page.

Xo

Jess

Jessica Weaver, CFP®, CDFA™, CFS®
Wealth Advisor

54 Grove Street Suite 2A
Somerville, NJ 08876

732-752-9191

The information contained in this book does not purport to be a complete description of the securities, markets, or developments referred to in this material. The information has been obtained from sources considered to be reliable, but we do not guarantee that the foregoing material is accurate or complete. Any information is not a complete summary or statement of all available data necessary for making an investment decision and does not constitute a recommendation. Any opinions of the chapter authors are those of the chapter author and not necessarily those of RJFS or Raymond James. Expressions of opinion are as of the initial book publishing date and are subject to change without notice.

Raymond James Financial Services, Inc. is not responsible for the consequences of any particular transaction or investment decision based on the content of this book. All financial, retirement and estate planning should be individualized as each person's situation is unique. Raymond James and its advisors do not offer tax or legal advice. You should discuss any tax or legal matters with the appropriate professional.

Securities offered through Raymond James Financial Services, Inc. Member FINRA/SIPC. Investment advisory services are offered through Raymond James Financial Services Advisors, Inc. Foran Financial Group is not a registered broker dealer and is independent of Raymond James Financial Services.

Links are being provided for information purposes only. Raymond James is not affiliated with and does not endorse, authorize or sponsor any of the listed websites or their respective sponsors. Raymond James is not responsible for the content of any website or the collection or use of information regarding any website's users and/or members.

Raymond James is not affiliated with and does not endorse the entities or persons mentioned above.

The examples listed in this book are hypothetical and for illustration purposes only. Actual investor results will vary.

Investing involves risk and you may incur a profit or loss regardless of strategy selected.

Certified Financial Planner Board of Standards, Inc. owns the certification marks CFP®, CERTIFIED FINANCIAL PLANNER™, CFP ® (with plaque design) and CFP ® (with flame design) in the U.S., which it awards to individuals who successfully complete CFP Board's initial and ongoing certification requirements.

Made in the USA
Middletown, DE
21 June 2019